W9-APM-392

## ABOUT THE AUTHORS

MARGARET ATHEY, classroom music specialist, is presently working in the schools of Shawnee Mission, Kansas. She helped to author their acclaimed *Elementary Music Curriculum* and has served on numerous committees in behalf of better music education. Her teaching experience has spanned all grade levels, with particular emphasis in elementary music and choral work.

GWEN HOTCHKISS is the Coordinator of Elementary Music for the Shawnee Mission, Kansas Public Schools. She is a specialist in curriculum development and instruction, and is an experienced classroom music, band and strings teacher at the elementary level. Other teaching experiences have included college level Humanities and Teacher Education Courses as well as flute and piccolo instruction. Both authors have previously collaborated on another highly successful book from Parker Publishing: *A Galaxy of Games for the Music Class*.

recognizing different composers and their music.

You'll also see how to plan and implement a number of innovative small group activities like—

- "Rotation Day" where students are challenged to learn a variety of musical concepts during specified time periods
- "Project Day" where each group develops and presents a student-created project
- "Performance Day" where newly discovered musical skills are shared through group performances

In addition, the guide contains an Instant Activity Locator that briefly describes each project and tells you the number of students required, the kinds of equipment needed, and the results you can expect from individual students as well as small groups.

Here, in short, is the one guide you need when it comes to providing your students with a more challenging and stimulating exposure to the wonderful world of music.

# Treasury of
## Individualized Activities
## for the Music Class

Previous books by the authors . . .

*A Galaxy of Games for the Music Class*

# Treasury of
# Individualized Activities
# for the Music Class

*Gwen Hotchkiss and Margaret Athey*

BRIAR CLIFF COLLEGE
LIBRARY
SIOUX CITY, IOWA

*Parker Publishing Company, Inc.*

*West Nyack, New York*

© 1977, by

Gwen Hotchkiss and Margaret Athey

All rights reserved. No part of this
book may be reproduced in any form or
by any means, without permission in
writing from the publisher.

**Library of Congress Cataloging in Publication Data**

Hotchkiss, Gwen,
    Treasury of individualized activities for the music
class.

    Bibliography: p.
    Includes index.
    1.  School music--Instruction and study--United States.
I.  Athey, Margaret,          joint author.  II.  Title.
MT3.U5H68          780'.72973          77-7555
ISBN 0-13-930602-1

Printed in the United States of America

MT
3
.U5
H68

2964097

Dedicated with affection
and appreciation
to
Chicki, Eric, Lew, and Hotch
Brad, Phillip, Karen, Charles
and our parents
Rachel and Ernest Robb
Mabel and Otto Davis
Thanks for your support!

# What This Book Will Do for You

This book will provide you with a great variety of practical ideas and activities complete with instructions to help you select the "right way" to individualize and personalize the musical growth of your students. You will find small group activities as well as individual activities so that you can move away from more traditional classroom methods as your students become able to handle the new-found freedoms of individualized instruction.

This book also tackles and solves the greatest problem that faces the teacher of the individualized classroom, "How can I manage this system?" Complete plans are presented for arranging the room, selecting and using appropriate equipment, controlling the flow of traffic, and adjusting activities to create a less-than-deadly level of working sound.

Seventy-five tested strategies for small group activities are based on concepts for developing and reinforcing skills that encourage freedom of personal discovery and inquiry. One small group strategy, Rotation Day, is developed around particular activities, each to be completed within an imposed time limit. Other exciting activities using small groups are Project Day, for integrating the arts through the development and presentation of student-created projects, and Performance Day, where newly learned musical skills are shared.

Over 300 individualized strategies in this book cover the development, preparation, implementation, and evaluation of both Learning Packets and Individualized Contracts. Actual examples for immediate use are given along with many additional ideas for the creative teacher to develop. Nearly 100 specific activities and ideas are presented for effectively creating an "open" classroom, as you develop Experience Centers in your classroom or around the building using those "fringes of time" when students have finished their work early or when the eager, highly motivated student is ready for a new challenge. Dozens of projects for use outside the school are also included here to add a "plus" to your students' musical environment.

Complete plans for implementation and evaluation are presented for nearly 500 activities. Each activity can be used as described here. In addition, you will no doubt want to develop and evaluate your own activities using these as a starting point.

As music educators, we are personally acquainted with the problems you face in the music room and have, in this book, given the keys to developing a program for successfully individualizing instruction through alternate activities to group instruction, as well as a bonanza of specific "how-to" helps including hundreds of tested activities.

*Gwen Hotchkiss*
*Margaret Athey*

# Table of Contents

# Instant Activity Locator

| Activity | No. of Students | Equipment | Result | Page |
|---|---|---|---|---|
| Writing a Song Parody | 3-6 | paper/pencil | performance | 54 |
| Making a Song Variation | 3-6 | familiar songs | performance | 54 |
| Singing with Accompaniment | 3-6 | familiar songs | performance | 55 |
| Accompanying with Two Rhythms | 3-6 | instruments familiar songs | performance | 55 |
| Creating a Twelve-Tone Row | 3-6 | resonator bells manuscript paper pencils | performance | 56 |
| Sound Piece with Sentences | 3-6 | sentences | performance | 56 |
| Creating an Opera | 3-6 | none or as desired | performance | 57 |
| Dramatizing a Ballad | 3-6 | familiar songs | performance | 58 |
| Creating a Penta-tonic Composition | 3-6 | bells, pencils manuscript paper | performance | 59 |
| Playing, Dancing or Singing | 3-6 | as required | performance | 59 |
| Pop Music Dance | 3-6 | record player recording | performance | 64 |
| Classical Music Dance | 3-6 | record player recording | performance | 64 |
| Singing Puppets | 3-6 | record player | performance | 64 |

| Activity | No. of Students | Equipment | Result | Page |
|---|---|---|---|---|
| | | headphones worksheets pencils | | |
| Classical Music Listening Station | 3-6 | record player recording headphones worksheets pencils | completed worksheet | 92 |
| Performers' Station | 3-6 | vertical file worksheets pencils | completed worksheets | 94 |
| Composers' Station | 3-6 | reference materials worksheets pencils | completed worksheets | 94 |
| Instrument Info Station | 3-6 | worksheets pencils reference materials | completed worksheets | 96 |
| Diatonic Bell Station | 3-6 | 6 diatonic bells with mallets bell task cards (pp. 98-100) | ensemble | 98 |
| Autoharp Station | 3-6 | 2 or 3 tuned autoharps autoharp task cards (pp. 101-102) | ensemble | 100 |
| Piano Station | 3-6 | 2 pianos piano task cards (pp. 103-108) | ensemble | 103 |
| Recorder Station | 3-6 | 6 recorders recorder fingering-chart disinfectant recorder task cards (pp. 109-110) | ensemble | 108 |
| Music Game Resources | 3-6 | games as desired | skill drill | 110 |
| "Orchestra Pit" | | prepared cards | naming instruments | 110 |

| Activity | No. of Students | Equipment | Result | Page |
|---|---|---|---|---|
| "Musical Perquackey" | | prepared cube | naming notes | 111 |
| "Rhythm Bowl" | | prepared tubes small ball | computing rhythms | 111 |
| "Before the Fall" | | prepared note cards floor staff | naming notes | 112 |
| "Musical Yahtze" | | prepared cube prepared game sheet | writing rhythms | 113 |
| "War-on-Notes" | | prepared cards | recognizing rhythmic notation | 113 |
| "Spin a Sonata" | | prepared spinner prepared score sheet | ordering a Sonata Form | 114 |
| Action Day | class in small groups | as desired | variation on Rotation Day | 115 |
| Half Steps in Music | 1-6 | prepared packet | a paper or a performance | 124 |
| Whole Steps in Music | 1-6 | prepared packet | a paper or a performance | 127 |
| Distinguishing Half Steps and Whole Steps | 1-6 | prepared packet | a paper or a performance | 128 |
| Major Scales | 1-6 | prepared packet | a paper or a performance | 129 |
| Chords | 1-6 | prepared packet | a paper or a performance | 131 |
| Orchestral Instruments | 1-6 | prepared packet | a paper or a performance | 132 |
| Tape Recorder Music | 1-6 | prepared packet | a paper or a presentation | 133 |
| "Till Eulenspiegel" | 1-6 | prepared packet | a paper or a presentation | 135 |

| Activity | No. of Students Equipment | Result | Page |
|---|---|---|---|
| Music Math | | wall display | 186 |
| Music Stories | | wall display | 187 |
| Music in the News | | wall display or bulletin board | 187 |
| Instrument Investigator | | wall display | 188 |
| Musical Maps | | wall display | 189 |
| Instrument Families | | Action Bulletin Board | 193 |
| Arrange the Notes | | Action Bulletin Board | 193 |
| Arrange the Terms | | Action Bulletin Board | 194 |
| Arrange the Instruments | | Action Bulletin Board | 194 |
| Name Keyboard Instruments | | Action Bulletin Board | 195 |
| Which Voice Is the Right Voice? | | Action Bulletin Board | 195 |
| Match the Symbol | | Action Bulletin Board | 196 |
| Which Nation Was My Home? | | Action Bulletin Board | 196 |
| Find a Mistake | | Action Bulletin Board | 196 |
| Place the Barlines | | Action Bulletin Board | 197 |
| Experience Centers | | table displays | 198 |
| Take-Home Teasers | | wall display | 199 |
| Folk Instruments: Scrambled Words | | | 199 |
| Music in Concert: Scrambled Words | | | 200 |
| Music Symbol Dot to Dot | | | 201 |
| Flower Notes: Color by Notes | | | 202 |
| Holiday Composer Names | | | 202 |
| Musical Instruments: Word Search | | | 203 |

*If a man does not keep pace with his companions, perhaps it is because he hears a different drummer. Let him step to the music which he hears, however measured or far away . . .*

Thoreau

# 1

## How to Develop an Individualized Learning Program for Music

*I hear and I forget*
*I see and I remember*
*I do and I understand.*

Chinese Proverb

Individualized learning is instruction that leads the student along a guided pathway through the channels of discovery and inquiry. The student begins at his own level of ability and is allowed to progress at his own rate. The student may also be permitted to choose his learning activity from several that are offered. Flexibility for both the teacher and student are built into the instruction to insure a personalization and humanization of the learning process. An "individualized" learning process may be interpreted to mean almost any learning technique in which the entire class is not participating in the same activity at the same time.

### EXPLORING THE NEED TO CHANGE TRADITIONAL MUSIC CLASSES

Music class has traditionally been oriented toward the group, paced by the teacher, and scheduled for administrative convenience. Student participation has often been limited to "looking and hearing," rather than "seeing and doing." Yet it has been found that the ability to learn music increases in direct proportion to a student's involvement with his personal learning process. Consequently, the student needs to be guided into making some of the decisions involving his alternative course of educational action. The desire to learn through involvement and participation must arise from within the student since musical learning is not something which can be accomplished for or given to another.

Because students learn by uniquely different patterns, a single method of instruction is not always effective. A wide spectrum of educational alternatives should be developed to permit each student to progress in a manner that complements his own style of learning. This book will show you how to develop learning alternatives for your music class, and it will provide many tested ideas for implementing them.

## HOW TO BEGIN AN INDIVIDUALIZED ADVENTURE IN MUSIC

The adoption of individualized alternatives in music class should not begin abruptly. You should know exactly where the class is headed through goals and objectives and have a thorough knowledge of the students before you begin.

### Student Readiness

Individualizing without "student readiness" may be disastrous. Peter, one of our students, is an example of a student who was not ready for the responsibility of individualization. Coming into school at midterm, he was totally bewildered at being asked to work something out for himself in the music class. While the other students gladly chose one project from the suggested list of ten, Peter was constantly at the teacher's side: "What does this mean?" "How can I?" "Is this O.K.?" He required much guidance, help, and reassurance before he could function successfully in the class. Imagine a whole class of students like Peter!

To develop student "readiness," freedom should be extended gradually while responsibilities are increased at the same time. For example, students can begin by selecting teacher-designed activities and gradually learn to work in small groups. Some of the early stages of individualizing may make use of one or more of the suggestions from

Small Group Activities, as presented in Chapters 3, 4, and 5. A traditional music class can begin gradually by working in Small Group Activities early in the school year and moving on to individual projects as the students are ready. For example, Mrs. Dobbs used this gradual approach in her sixth grade music classroom. She began in September using the last Friday of the month for a Small Group Activity. At first, she designed the activities and the students chose from them. As the semester progressed, the students who were "ready" to increase responsibility began to help in designing their own activities in the small groups. Ted and John were very mature, so Mrs. Dobbs expanded their instruction to the Learning Packet Activities (Chapter 6). These boys really thrived on working beyond the scope of the group. The old sixth grade blues had disappeared from this music class.

From realizing success in the Small Group Activities, the student can go on to Individualized Activities, such as those found in Chapter 8, "Environment-Plus Projects." As he becomes more confident, the student will be ready for gradually proceeding toward Learning Packets (Chapter 6) and then into Individual Contracts (Chapter 7). Mrs. Nolte, for example, observed that after three or four months of Small Group Activities, her students were ready for Learning Packet Activities. She used her usual curriculum as she developed the packets. Her class became so interested in the packets on the American musical theater that they planned a field trip to see a stage show. Several girls developed their own show and were chosen to present it to the first grade. For Mrs. Nolte, the crowning glory was the Patriotic Musical that was planned by her sixth grade, a class which had previously been "turned off" by music!

## Student Attitudes

A consideration of equal importance to "readiness" in planning activities is an awareness of the students' attitudes toward music and toward themselves. The teacher must be aware of the individual differences among students and strive to create a non-threatening, friendly atmosphere in which all can learn. By carefully observing a music class as a group of individuals, the teacher will discover many facts that affect students' attitudes toward each other as well as toward the music class. Observing and chatting with the students in the playground, lunchroom, halls, and other school settings, helps reinforce individualism and aids in developing a positive attitude toward the music teacher. Occasionally, the opportunity arises to hold music class in a different classroom; the change of location is an aid to individualism. Talking with classroom teachers and other specialists concerning a specific student or situation gives a new perspective to a class. Through music, students can be encouraged to learn to accept other students as individuals. A free exchange of ideas concerning musical happenings should be encouraged in the music classroom to create a friendly atmosphere. The structure of Talent Shows, Sharing Days, or any performance time also helps create a positive response within the musical peer group.

The acceptance of the peer group was achieved through the Talent Show when Peggy, a sixth grade girl who had little regard for herself as a human being, realized that she could make a positive contribution to the class. Her parents were too busy to give her any attention at home, and in order to receive the attention she craved, she had developed a pattern of loud, boisterous behavior. She had become a real problem during music class by criticizing everyone. The teacher, Miss Davis, could more easily view Peggy's individual problems when the class worked in small groups, and she began to analyze Peggy's personality problem in relation to her work. With great care, Peggy was guided in choosing an appropriate companion to work with; and gradually, through the use of positive reinforcement along with the increase in learning responsibility, Peggy was able to make an appropriate contribution to her music class. Her new-found attitude helped in other school situations as well.

## Motivating Students

Teachers need to help students succeed since success is motivated by success. Students should be permitted to follow their own interests in learning situations that involve performance. Their self-esteem will be increased by public recognition of a real learning accomplishment. In the case of ten-year-old Scott, for example, it happened that his very first success came when he sang with two other boys in a small group on Performance Day. The student response was so pleasing to Scott, a typical fifth-grader, that he was willing after that to sing a solo for the class. A business-like approach to singing had brought him more recognition than any amount of "showing-off."

You can be helpful by seeing and encouraging a student's potential. Most students are eager to apply themselves when they feel that as a result of their labors they are creating things successfully. A student who feels good about himself will have the confidence to experiment further.

## Creating a New Role for the Music Teacher

Individualization in the music class should result in a new state of mind for you, the teacher. Instead of being simply a dispenser of knowledge, the role has changed to one of guiding, consulting, diagnosing, evaluating, or conferring, but never dominating the learning process.

You can make available to your students many types of learning materials. When there is only time available for two lessons in which to present the "Life and Works of Mozart," what can be done? The traditional teacher may choose a few songs to sing, a story to tell, and some music literature to present. In the individualized classroom, you may announce the topic and the available materials and then have the class pursue the materials of their choice either individually or in small groups. At the end of the second day, a spokesman from each group may share what has been learned about Mozart.

In following this approach, one seventh-grade teacher, Mr. Heinz, changed his role from that of a lecturer into one of a planner, a developer of teaching materials, and an organizer of classroom equipment and space. He spent two days as a careful listener in the classroom, giving guidance where needed and inserting provocative questions with precise timing. He also noted in the record book any significant behavior problems or exceptional growth of individual students. During this time, Mr. Heinz exchanged ideas on a one-to-one basis with far more students than would have been possible in the traditional music class. He was generous with praise and noted individuals who took initiative as well as those who did not. Mozart had helped to create a pleasant opportunity for the teacher to facilitate some learning. Mozart himself might have been pleased!

## INDIVIDUALIZATION AS A PART OF THE TOTAL MUSIC PROGRAM

Music at the elementary level is basically a sharing activity. It would not be much fun to listen to tapes, write evaluations, or respond to a designated recording at the exclusion of all other experiences. Ac-

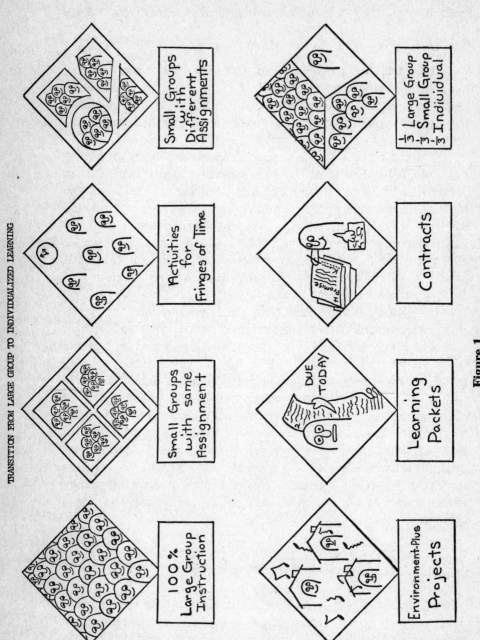

Figure 1

tivities such as singing, playing instruments, and creating movement are vitally important and sometimes work best in large group activities. Large group activities must not be neglected and should ideally comprise about 50 percent of the total music time. In this respect, music is one of the few disciplines where every student may work cooperatively to create a greater whole. This process is vital to the development of the total child.

## Easing Smoothly into an Individualized Music Program

Small group activities and individual projects lend themselves easily to such things as practicing skills and reinforcing concepts. In Figure 1 it can be seen how the traditional music class may gradually evolve into the open classroom. If the teacher uses this diagram as a step-by-step process and acts as a critical observer at each step along the way, the process of developing alternate activities for the music class should be an exciting and stimulating adventure.

After following the step-by-step procedure from the traditional large group instruction to individualized learning, a middle school teacher, Miss Roper, felt particularly well rewarded after her class developed a complete unit on rock music. The class had determined their own goals and developed and completed their contracts. The greatest surprise of all was George, who had been such a problem at mid-year. George organized his own rock group, and the group performed in the All-School Talent Show. Looking on with great pride, Miss Roper was sure that Individualized Learning Activities provided one answer to music education for the youth of today.

# 2

## *How to Structure the Environment for Alternate Activities in the Music Classroom*

*The musician may sing to you of the rhythm which is in all space, but he cannot give you the ear which arrests the rhythm nor the voice that echoes it.*

Gibran

Establishing a new learning environment is not abandoning familiar ways, but building and establishing new structures within the music classroom to encourage a new style of learning. You, the teacher, will need to change the environment in order to allow *students* to assume the responsibility for learning. Creating a more spontaneous environment can help convince the student that he is perceived in a new light, thus helping to give him a greater sense of responsibility. It is important for old structures to be replaced with new ones in order to avoid chaos. Students who are expected to work without the support of any structure will not be free but will be bound by their immediate interests and impulses.

## HOW TO CREATE AN "ELECTRIC" ENVIRONMENT

An exciting, electrifying environment is essential to the motivation and stimulation of each student as an individual.

### Flexibility Is the Key

Spontaneity and flexibility are the key environmental factors for encouraging curiosity about new ways to learn. Qualities of initiative, independence, and confidence in accepting responsibility can only develop in an atmosphere of freedom and understanding. First, you should establish a solid framework of instructional goals to insure the flexibility of an internal structure of activities. While it is seemingly a paradox, it is nevertheless true that to have less inner structure takes more careful planning and evaluation of the outer structures. This planning is necessary to allow greater flexibility in development of the student alternatives. You must plan sufficiently to be ready at all times for any worthwhile, even if unpredictable, tangent that warrants pursuit and encouragement. Flexibility of the planning process is only one factor. In true individualization, the facilities, schedules, and group sizes, as well as materials, also need to be flexible to allow for variety and individual differences. To make a music classroom really come to life and electrify the learner, the classroom structure must be flexible!

### Ground Rules for Management

A simple set of ground rules should suffice to make any classroom manageable. Teachers sometimes feel that involving students in a different setting and using different materials is an invitation to chaos. On the contrary, when students become actively involved in investigating a problem, more low-keyed noise may exist, but the usual disruptive elements are almost non-existent. Mrs. Robb had her class help set the ground rules for class work habits. She was surprised to find that the same students who were usually disruptive were the ones who offered the most suggestions on developing good cooperative work rules. For example, one student, Tony, was unusually annoying in classwork; he interrupted and argued with other students during a regular large group class. After he gave several excellent suggestions, Mrs. Robb asked

Tony why he didn't use these ideas for himself. By soliciting specific suggestions from her class, Mrs. Robb had made her students directly accountable for their own ground rules. Students such as Tony will develop a greater respect for the class once the management process belongs to them.

### Central Focus on the Student

In any type of individualized instruction, the environment must focus on the student. The classroom reflects this by creating ways for the student to have an opportunity to make decisions and become actively involved in his area of interest. An environment that is functioning well does not need to have the teacher standing at attention continually. You should listen carefully to every student and encourage ideas as they develop the thinking-learning process. Mr. Coleman discovered that by responding to student inquiries through interspersing additional questions, he stimulated a real spark in classroom discussions. In one student-oriented discussion of Beethoven's *Pastoral Symphony*, the students became involved with Beethoven's love of nature. Further student discussion created an empathy for Beethoven's hearing impairment and then led to the importance of finding solitude before composing creatively. Another day of discussion developed around other composers who used nature in composition. Mr. Coleman was excited to see some obvious intellectual growth occurring in his music class. The students enjoyed sharing their ideas and knew that Mr. Coleman really cared about them and their message.

### Use of Multi-Sensory Experiences

To keep the environment exciting, a variety of multi-sensory experiences should be sequentially developed to assist the student in learning to express the language of music. These sensory stimuli play an important part in the motivation of a student and contribute to the passive-active process of learning. Multi-sensory stimuli such as attractive, learning-packed bulletin boards and a variety of eye-catching charts are important for reinforcement. Materials to manipulate, feel, work with, or build, and a great variety of music to hear can help sharpen perception. A student's ability to perceive and discriminate is directly related to his involvement in his own skill development. As a student increases his musical skills, he develops a more positive attitude not only toward music but toward himself as well.

## HOW TO ORGANIZE FOR ALTERNATE ACTIVITIES

The physical features of the music room (space and materials) are not the only important factors in the organization of a room for individualization—time and lesson content should be considered as well.

### Organizing the Instructional Time

A sense of instructional timing is as vital to the individualized structure as it is for the large group. In a large group situation, you should pace your class with activities which are fast-slow-fast-slow-fast (ABABA) to keep interest and enthusiasm at a peak. Each segment should be carefully timed to insure the greatest area of concentration in the slower portion of each lesson. Harry, one of Mrs. Rowland's class athletes, remarked that calling the planned structure by letters (ABABA) or numbers (121) at the beginning of the class reminded him of his football plays. This excited him as well as other sports-minded friends, and for Mrs. Rowlands it was sheer magic. Another teacher, Ms. Freeman, adapted a similar pattern for organizing her time as she developed her individualized instruction. She started the class with a large group activity, such as singing, rhythms, or a relevant review. Following this segment, students were divided into small groups to individualize skills which would reinforce the total lesson objective. The last part of the lesson was a return to the large group, at which time the small groups performed and shared their newly learned skills. The students thrived on the variety of structures and became more highly motivated. For organization of time when she was using units more in-depth, Mrs. Bowers augmented the form by using large group work one day, small group work the second day, and a return to the large group for sharing and discussion on the third. Mrs. Bowers found that all of her students enjoyed knowing the daily plans for the unit before delving into the subject. A total learning environment for alternate activities should be carefully timed to encourage independent thought in a systematic order.

### Organizing the Lesson Content

The easiest method to use in organizing the music lesson content is the concept approach. After isolating a specific goal-related concept from your curriculum guide or basic textbook, you should carefully plan the learning environment by limiting the centers of activity and gearing the selected materials toward the chosen concept. A skillfully planned learning environment can arouse curiosity and entice the learners to explore and experiment. In this environment, students can develop self-motivation and self-discipline to discover and find answers to their own questions and problems. Mrs. Kenney always cringed when the curricular unit on the twelve-tone row appeared. It seemed to her that about one-fourth of the class never really understood the music. Using the concept approach toward individualizing the lesson content, she began by presenting a brief large group discussion-demonstration on the "sound" of the twelve-tone row and the "uses" of it. The "how" was turned into small group work so that the exploration and experimentation belonged to the students. Four activity centers were set up around the music room. Each center contained concise directions for creating and developing a twelve-tone row along with the necessary resonator bells. Since their number of bells was limited, a fifth group of students solved the problem by volunteering to compose a sixteen-beat percussion segment to be played as an introduction and "bridge" between the "rows." The class enjoyed the "Row Rondo" so much that they invited their school principal to attend a mini-performance. Individualization of the twelve-tone row had given an entirely new perspective to the sixth grade curriculum.

Consider the activities you will be doing over the next instructional period. The period will probably include some units which would profit from small group or individualized study.

## Organizing the Music Room

Your music room reflects your idea of who is responsible. Visually decentralizing the room can honestly be very difficult for some teachers who have become accustomed to "their things." Classrooms differ considerably, with each one reflecting the teacher's special interests and areas of competency. You can learn to become more student-oriented by continually observing and responding to students and gradually evolving into a new style. A careful examination of the music room will help determine what children need in order to learn, and then you must have the courage to control the environment for the sake of learning. After observing and diagnosing the students' behavior, a skillful teacher can combine knowledge gleaned to facilitate learning.

The music classroom can be divided by:

- area rugs
- pillows (especially large ones)
- book cases
- easels
- large boxes (from appliance stores)
- window shades on frames
- movable storage units
- pianos
- coat racks
- curtains

Instructional information or exhibits can be adhered to the dividers as a sound control feature. All dividers should be strategically placed so that the teacher has a clear view of the entire room.

In the total plan, remember to include a place for large group activities and these:

- Quiet activity areas
  (reading, listening, research, worksheets)
- Noisier activity areas
  (game table, discussion areas)
- Conference area
- Laboratory area
  (making instruments, composing music, playing instruments)
- Storage area
  (materials and supplies for student use)
- Adequate spaces between areas to allow for a free flow of traffic

There are a multitude of ways to place the furniture in your music room to better facilitate individualized instruction. If you are beginning your transition from a large group to small groups, you may choose Figure 2. This placement can accomodate a large group instructional area with satellite individualized areas; or small group work may be done in the peripheral areas while the center area is used for remedial larger group work.

This same setting can also be used by the teacher who uses individualized techniques with some class groups and large group techniques with others.

When you begin to use small group structures, Figure 3 may be

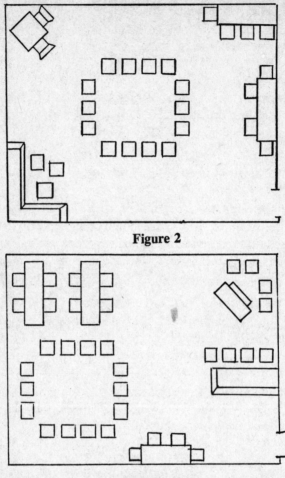

**Figure 2**

**Figure 3**

useful. The small group areas may be used for laboratory experiences, learning packets, Action Day, Project Day, or Performance Day as well as other types of small group study.

There can be as many individualized areas in the music classroom as there are student projects. You can use all of the corners of your room, the school media center facilities, listening stations in the library, and learning centers throughout the entire school. You may want to utilize the center area of your room for large groups and the outer areas for individualized projects, or you may want to individualize the entire room on certain days, as shown in Figure 4.

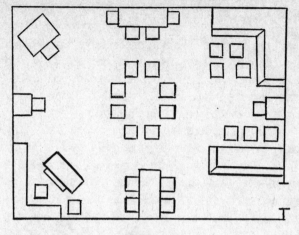

**Figure 4**

Regardless of the formation of your music room, it must be colorful and cheerful in appearance and spontaneous in character.

## *Developing the Instructional Materials*

Since many materials are necessary in creating individualized instruction, you will probably need to have students develop some of their own. So that cost or lack of ready-prepared teacher materials does not become a factor, it is necessary to keep alert to the multitude of no-cost materials.

Here are some no-cost materials you can make use of:

- magazines
- music industry catalogues
- old music textbooks
- newspapers
  (articles on musicians, musical events, aleatoric music, stock market reports for sound compositions, and so on)
- maps
  (locations of events or composers, charting progress, music/social studies, and so on)
- used tapes
- records from local radio stations
- scrap items for making instructional materials and games

## Establishing a New Social Environment

By changing the physical environment of your music room, you are establishing a new social environment as well. Socially, a need to help and share will supersede the atmosphere of competition. In this new environment a respect will develop among the students not only for each other, but also for materials and equipment.

New external procedures do not cure internal problems, however. No amount of careful room arrangment will cure a weak or unhealthy classroom. As new habits are developed and new attitudes toward learning are adopted, both the teacher and the student may see the need to change structures again. Learning areas should change as the needs change, but caution should be exercised in altering learning areas too frequently or some of the familiar visual cues that students depend upon for security will be gone and confusion will result. Every six to ten weeks a regrouping of the class, the space, and the equipment, along with a change in media, will serve as a check on your operational plans.

## Organizing for Individual Social Needs

Remember that some children are able to function best in large groups only. When this is the case, the opportunity to work in small groups or on individualized activities can be offered as a reward for good work in the large group activity. Some students can work individually only after they have been specifically placed and given definite assigned tasks. For these students, the room can be used similarly to the one in which the teacher is in the process of making the transition from a large group to small groups (Figure 2).

## HOW TO DEVELOP
## STUDENT PROGRESS CONFERENCES

Student-teacher conferences are a proven way to develop effective communications throughout the learning experience. The music teacher in the position of having little personal contact with the student will find it greatly advantageous to plan for conferences on a regular basis. Such conferences will provide an opportunity for getting better acquainted, establishing rapport, and charting musical progress, as well as helping to solve a student's personal problems by being a good listener. Effective communication is a vital part of the learning process.

## Creating an Atmosphere for the Conference

Preparing a time for each student to have a personal conference is an important part of the individualization process. The atmosphere for the conference needs to be casual to allow a free exchange of ideas. You will find this a quiet-private time for you and your students as you become better acquainted with their ideas. To help create this atmosphere you might want to place a small table and chairs in the sunny corner of your music room. At the conference time, a bowl of peppermints for the table further creates a "chatting" atmosphere. Discussions during these conference times help to motivate musical growth and are a very important personal occasion for both you and your students.

## Understanding the Purpose of the Conference

There are several reasons for scheduling a student conference. Each personal contact should have a definite purpose, and these purposes vary from time to time and from student to student.

### Personal progress conferences

The Personal Progress Conference should emphasize progress of the student but also should reflect the way a student perceives himself and his position in relationship to the class. This type of conference is for sharing an evaluation; but to be effective, it must be a discussion involving interest surveys, anecdotal records, diagnostic tests, mastery tests, and a charting of musical progress. Motivation toward learning musical skills can be coerced by the extrinsic reward of a letter grade, but the development of the total student is more important. Grades alone do very little toward behavior modification since behavior is a symptom of internal value. The conferences work on this internal value by comparing a student to himself rather than to his peer group. Occasionally a teacher-parent-student conference is important to encourage a student or to share successes.

### Planning conferences

A Planning Conference may be needed to develop the next instructional goal with a student. These conferences are generally necessary for the exceptional student who develops ahead of the regular scope of activities or for the slower student who needs a special incentive. During these conferences, interests are discussed and objectives leading toward achievement of the desired goal are established.

### Check-point conferences

A Check-Point Conference is short in duration and is used for the teacher to oversee the progress of a completed goal. A student can quickly share a success and check-in for a "go ahead" toward the next goal. These conferences should be held the same day of the student accomplishment and may be during class. These brief conferences help show the student that you are interested in his daily progress, and they have high motivational value.

### Attitudinal conferences

You can request an Attitudinal Conference to establish a better rapport with a specific student or to become better acquainted with his musical interests. There are times when a student, by his attitude, signals loneliness, lack of motivation, and a need for teacher support. These conferences are generally short and an excellent time to show your support for the student and his musical progress. During these Attitudinal Conferences many things can be learned about the students and how they perceive the class. You can quickly determine what the students feel they need to know about music and with this information balance your instruction with the results from sessions in skill testing. You may also discover, much to your surprise, how you are perceived as their teacher. It is not uncommon for some students to really enjoy you as a person, but when you begin "preaching" they will tune you out. Although at first this may seem hard to comprehend, this simple revelation can result in improved teaching.

All of these conferences require accountability on the part of the teacher and the student. The student learns quickly that the important requisites for the privilege of freedom are responsibility for one's own conduct and responsibility for learning. Along with this the student must respect the rights of others, their possessions, their beliefs, and their creations.

## Scheduling the Conferences

The conferences may take place during music class time while other students are working in small groups or individually. To emphasize the student's responsibility in the scheduling of the conference, you might try posting a list of available times by using a sign-up sheet system for student-teacher appointments. By using this sign-up system, and by using part of the music class while the rest of the class is working in Small Group Activities, you can have conferences with an entire sixth grade class of 28 students during any month. The frequency of conferences and the length of them will vary from student to student as well as with what the occasion demands. For some students a monthly conference will be necessary; some may require after-school conferences; and many students may need conferences only once each semester.

| SIGN UP FOR PERSONAL MUSIC CONFERENCE | | | |
|---|---|---|---|
| Homeroom Teacher | | | |
| Class meeting time: 8:50 - 9:30 | | | |
|  | Monday | Wednesday | Friday |
| 9:00 |  |  |  |
| 9:04 |  |  |  |
| 9:08 |  |  |  |
| 9:12 |  |  |  |
| 9:16 |  |  |  |

**Figure 5: Sample Sign-up Sheet**

## HOW TO ORGANIZE STUDENT EVALUATION TO PREVENT THE PAPER MONSTER

Effective and efficient management procedures are important to the success of the individualized program. A definite system should be established for charting musical progress, but if you assume all of the responsibility for the evaluation, you have created an all-consuming paper monster.

## Time Saving Procedures

Any individualized system needs a procedure which is firmly established and easily managed by the students. Each student needs to take the responsibility for his progress. If the student goals have been securely established (realistic, simple, and firm) the student will be able to care for most of the system.

### Student self-evaluation

Student self-evaluation is effective for activities related to a specific goal. If the teacher has established a progress continuum, the student will know where he is and can proceed independently. When he has reached a specific point on the continuum, he will be ready for a Check-Point Conference, then he can proceed along the continuum. When a student completes his specific goal, he can sign up for a new-content seminar or group discussion; or depending on the topic, he might decide to choose optional work toward the same goal. With students evaluating the activities, the teacher will evaluate the completion of the goal. This saves a great deal of time since the activities are the time-consuming area.

When a student creates his own project, he can evaluate the effectiveness of his materials and share with the class. For this type of evaluation, the class has profited from the experience, the student has learned from the project, and the presentation has saved teacher evaluation time.

### Buddy system

Students enjoy working in a buddy system where they choose or are assigned a partner. This is a good way to further reinforce a concept. There are occasions when a student who has finished more quickly can explain an activity to a slower student, or he might become a test-giver.

### Tutorial system

Tutoring students in lower grades or slower students within a class is a help to both the teacher and the student. It builds the confidence of the teaching student and develops a sense of responsibility toward learning. The tutored student enjoys working with his friend while he develops his musical proficiency.

### Human resources for assistance

If the teacher needs additional assistance, many schools use cadet assistants from the junior and senior high schools, teacher-aids, student teachers, or parent and grandparent volunteers. In utilizing human resources, both the student and the assistant profit in the learning process.

## Collecting the Data for Individualizing

Data can be collected from a variety of sources to chart a student's musical progress and to insure a deeper understanding of the total student.

### Diagnostic measurement

Information for diagnostic measurements can come from a standardized music test, from teacher-made tests covering specific materials, or from student-made tests. Student-constructed worksheets are a valuable system of testing, since they are developed at the student's level of understanding from his own interest and they serve as a self-diagnosis of the student's understanding of the content area.

### Interest analysis

Keeping in touch with students' personal preferences and interests is important in collecting data. This should be done frequently since interests change as maturity evolves. This can be done through a casual conversational method or by a teacher-developed questionnaire.

### Various work and media

Students should be observed in a variety of work situations and using a variety of media for learning. From these teacher observations would probably come the daily "grade" for each student.

### Mastery tests

At the completion of a given unit, it is valuable to test the student's knowledge or mastery of the material.

Parts or all of these methods for collecting data may be used to successfully individualize your music class.

## *Recording the Data*

Data collected from daily studies can be recorded by both teachers and students by using a file-folder system, an index-card system, a wall-chart system, and the teacher's record book. The combination of collected data can be used during conference time as they plan new goals and evaluate student progress.

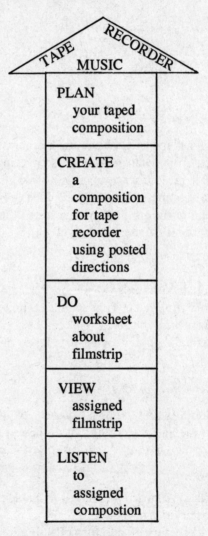

**Figure 6**

### Individual progress reports

An individual may chart his daily progress simply by checking (√) a designated blank to show completion of an assigned task or, more elaborately, by writing a report to cover content area, creating a composition using skills which have been learned, developing an experiment to demonstrate a principle learned, and sharing with the class.

### Individual charting of progress

Students can also keep track of their daily progress by using a personal marker on a wall chart designed to indicate progressive movement toward goal accomplishment. Figure 6 shows how a student can be charted individually as he colors each phase of his rocket upon completion of a segment of instruction.

### Group charting of progress

If a greater degree of group motivation is desired, a system of charting total group accomplishment by small groups or by individuals may be desired. Small groups working together may move their personal marker on a wall chart designed to indicate progressive movement toward goal accomplishment in competition with other small groups. If individual charting is desired, the same system may be used by substituting individual names for small group names. Figure 7 shows how small groups may be charted individually within a group chart as they move their rocket vertically through the grid toward completion of the goal.

### Goals task card

The Goals Task Card system may be used for small group work or individualized work during completion of activities, learning packets, or contracts. If you use a key-punch type card, an entire class may be checked instantly for completion of activities or tasks. As each assignment is completed, a notch must be cut from the edge of the card to the hole-punch (see Figure 8). All of the student cards which indicate a completed activity or task will be notched, and they will not be caught by the pencil. The pencil will pull only cards of students who have not completed the task.

## PLAYING UKULELE

### (A Small Group Activity requiring several ukuleles)

| | | | | | | | |
|---|---|---|---|---|---|---|---|
| Move three spaces if you chose a three chord song | | | | | | | |
| Move two spaces if you chose a two chord song | | | | | | | |
| Move one space if you chose a one chord song | | | | | | | |
| Accompany the class while they sing your song | | | | | | | |
| Select and practice one song | | | | | | | |
| Create two ways of strumming a song you learned | | | | | | | |
| Play two songs from the three chord list | | | | | | | |
| Play two songs from the two chord list | | | | | | | |
| Play two songs from the one chord list | | | | | | | |

**Figure 7**

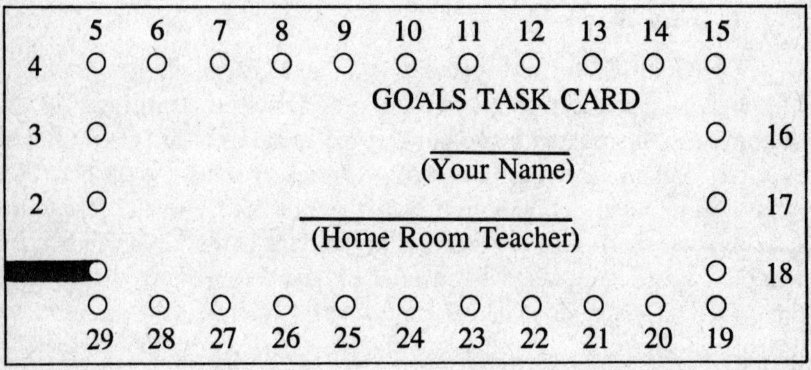

**Figure 8: Goals Task Card**

## HOW TO ADAPT THE SITUATION FOR
## THE TRAVELING MUSIC TEACHER

When the music teacher travels from classroom to classroom within one building or travels between buildings, the tendency to ignore the need to individualize is understandable. The mechanics of organizing such an instructional program may become more difficult. However, it is not impossible. The teacher must be persistent and determined if she is to motivate her students as well as herself to undertake an individualized project.

If you are a traveling music teacher, you will need to explore the school, seeking possible locations for instructional nooks.

### Temporary Centers for Individualized Units

Temporary learning centers can be cleverly devised in even the most unusual places. These centers can be developed around student interest or around skill development as diagnosed in the regular music class. Students can become involved in the process of planning by suggesting how many students there should be per learning center, deciding what materials are needed for each center, determining the evaluating criteria, or actually running the center. Centers might be located in:

- Hallways or corridors
- Moderate-sized storage rooms
- Small rooms
- Stairwells

### Permanent Centers for Individualized Units

Permanent centers can be set up in appropriate non-music classrooms by using prepared assignment cards. Some ideas to be considered are:

- Science-music center containing equipment for tuned glasses
- Science-music center containing equipment for producing sound tapes
- Art-music centers for exploring the humanities
- Bulletin boards in the hallways with news of concerts or artist performances

- Holiday centers presenting ways music is used for holidays in various countries
- Inter-curricular centers such as social studies or language arts with music
- Game centers for students who finish their work quickly
- Instrument centers (autoharp or guitar) to learn accompaniments for folk songs
- Record centers for listening to everything from the classics to pop-hits, with appropriate worksheets

### Media Centers for Individualized Units

Almost every elementary school has a media center located within the library area of the building. By developing units which involve media equipment within this area, you can eliminate the need to move equipment and find other locations. For example, you could set up:

- Listening centers using recordings
- Listening centers using tapes with study sheets to guide the instruction
- Filmstrip centers
- Reading centers containing books about composers, musicians, or music-related subjects

### Music Laboratories

The laboratory for musical exploration can be placed in any room where students can be free to personally explore an area of interest. Even among schools without a music room there is an occasional art-science room or student work room. Laboratories are generally areas where a greater sound level is acceptable. These may be used for:

- Taping sound compositions
- Building musical instruments
- Craft projects to reinforce music instruction
- Practicing instruments

### Equipment-Cart Centers

Most traveling music teachers are well-practiced in using a cart to carry equipment into the classroom. Why not make an Equipment-Cart

Learning Center? The cart could contain specific materials for the objective of the week and could be located at any convenient place. Materials appropriate for this center might be:

- Games for skill reinforcement
- Study material for a specific concept
- Worksheets for review
- Just-for-Fun papers

With some practice the traveling teacher can learn to capitalize on the movable environment and have the students develop the responsibility for preparing equipment. The schedule will be greatly eased without the pressure of moving the piano and books at every session, and some responsibility for learning will be placed on the students. The teacher must view individualizing instruction as a challenge and constantly strive to meet this challenge.

# 3

## Methods and Ideas
## for Performance Day

*The dominant note of education at
its beginning and its end is freedom,
but there is an intermediate state
of discipline.*

Alfred Whitehead
Philosopher

To prepare for a music class Performance Day, the class is divided into groups of from four to six students. Each group is given the same assignment. The assignment specifies a type of performance to be given. One or more days in class is allowed for preparing the performance, and on the designated Performance Day each group performs for the entire class.

## HOW TO PLAN FOR PERFORMANCE DAY

Possibilities for performance assignments are endless. Activities planned for Performance Day may be developed from music textbooks, from the regular music curriculum, or from student interest areas, and then they can be organized into a form usable in small group work. Some that have been used successfully are:

- Writing a song parody
- Making a song variation
- Singing a song with instrumental accompaniment
- Accompanying a song with two different rhythm patterns
- Creating a twelve-tone row
- Making a sound piece with sentences
- Making a sound piece with natural sounds
- Making a sound piece with vocal sounds
- Creating an instrumental ensemble

Performance Day is one of the easiest techniques to use in making a transition from large group to individualized instruction. You will find that introducing Performance Day is simple and that the students' response is usually positive. Plan the assignment carefully, give clearly stated instructions, and your students can function very well in small groups, though they may have had little or no previous experience with such groups.

## The Teacher's Function as Group Advisor

If the assignment is clearly spelled out, if the groups are firmly designated, if all necessary equipment is readily available, if the date of Performance Day is understood, then you can step aside and allow the students to get to work. You may then serve as advisor and counselor, as well as evaluator of work habits.

In working as the advisor, you need to encourage discussion in each small group. Discussion contributes to learning as well as to social development. A free exchange and sharing of information to bring about an orderly approach to problem solving is a necessity. Often during small group discussions, a new area of interest for study and research will emerge. You should observe the group to see if the designated leader really leads the group or if there is competition for this role. All group participants should develop skills in expressing themselves and listening while they are working on the specific objectives. At first students may be overly dependent on you—with questions such as, "What shall we do now?"—but as the students gain in confidence and responsibility these questions will diminish. Watch for the overly aggressive students, students who are unable to keep to the subject, those who dominate the group by competing for recognition, those who "horse around," and those who do not join in. Such problems should be dealt with on an individual basis.

## HOW TO IMPLEMENT PERFORMANCE DAY

### Forming the Groups

The activities which are suggested for Performance Day succeed best when the students work in groups of four, five, or six students. Many techniques may be used to divide the class into the groups.

- The chairs can be arranged in small groups before the students arrive. Where the students sit will determine group membership.
- If the assignment has been printed on a Spirit Master, the teacher may place color-coded marks on the reverse of each paper. After presenting the assignment, students could locate their colored mark and move to the spot in the room that has been designated for that particular color.
- The "numbering off" system is an old standby and is recommended. In this system, each student calls a number in order: one, two, three, four, or five. After each student has called a number, all the "ones" move to a designated area, the "twos" move to a designated area, and so on.
- Another time the teacher may want to appoint groups—"This row will be a group."
- Assign the groups by alphabetical order of student names.
- Develop a socio-gram to allow students to work with their choice of friends while maintaining control of an organized system. To develop a socio-gram, students make a list of five preferred classmates. The teacher then tallies all student preferences and organizes the groups correspondingly.
- Assign them according to ability levels.
- The teacher may simply say, "Get together with four others," and thus allow a free choice.

The main thing to remember in the business of formulating groups is that no one system should be used exclusively or with too much repetition. The system should vary frequently. Boys and girls may moan and groan at the outset, but they will survive it, and variety is important for them, too!

## Organizing the Group Members

Groups may be organized in one of the following ways.

### Tightly structured groups

In a Tightly Structured Group, each group member is assigned one of the following roles:

1. Captain (gets the group going and acts as leader)
2. Recorder (does any necessary writing)
3. Equipment Manager (handles all necessary equipment)
4. Clean-Up Manager (leaves work area tidy)
5. Observer (keeps group busy and aware of time limitations). He may serve also as evaluator.
6. File Clerk (does any necessary filing)

Group members may determine the role to be assumed by each member, or the roles may be assigned by the teacher. When a group has less than six members, these six responsibilities should be assumed by the existing group members. A list of these six roles with their respective job descriptions may be posted on the wall so that students can refer to them easily at all times.

### Loosely structured groups

In a Loosely Structured Group, the only assigned role is that of a Captain or Leader. His job is to be responsible for everyone and everything in the group. This Captain may be elected by group members or appointed by the teacher.

### Unstructured group

An Unstructured Group is one with absolutely no assigned roles. Usually in such a group, one person does emerge as having the "leading spirit" but, nevertheless, all are held equally responsible.

The teacher must determine with each new assignment which of these group structures to employ. That decision may be based on the following variable factors: complexity of assignment and time available for preparing the assignment.

Generally speaking, the Closely Structured Group is desirable for the complicated, time-consuming assignment, while the Loosely Structured Group with its teacher-appointed Captain may be best for a simple ten minute assignment. The success of the Unstructured Group may depend on how well the teacher knows the students. In some classes, Unstructured Groups may always be desirable, and in other classes, such groups may never work successfully. The teacher's knowledge of the students and their behavior patterns is vital to the success of any new venture.

### Peer Assessment of Group Work

Peer assessment of the work of each group member is desirable for every group experience. In the tightly Structured Group, the assessment may be given by the Observer; in the Loosely Structured Group, the assessment may be given by the Captain; and in the Unstructured Group, the teacher may appoint one member to give assessments at the end of the experience. In experimenting with different ways of accomplishing peer asssessment in small group endeavors, some teachers have concluded that the best way is also the simplest: "Did this group member help the group?" The student evaluator finds it easy to answer that question: "Yes, he had some good ideas," "Yes, she was very cooperative," or "No, he only banged on the bells and didn't help at all," "No, he was talking constantly and never listened." The class seems to feel respect for both the question and its answers. Consequently, we recommend using that one simple question as a stimulus for peer evaluation in each group experience: "Did (Mary) help the group?"

### Presenting the Assignment

It is necessary for the teacher to decide each time whether the assignment should be given before or after the groups are formulated. Circumstances and the nature of the assignment may make it necessary to vary this procedure from time to time. Suffice it to say that only after both things have been accomplished (presentation of assignment and formation of groups) can the work begin.

The Performance Day assignment may be written on the chalkboard, a chart, or a Spirit Master. The teacher should carefully present the assignment to the entire class and should be sure that the assignment is well understood before declaring the beginning of the work session. Nothing is more disastrous than a group of fifth graders with no clear idea of their assigned task!

Figure 9 is an example of a Performance Day assignment as it might appear on a Spirit Master.

Assignment:   Puppets Singing a Holiday Song

1. Choose a song from a holiday recording. (It should be one you know very well.)
2. Choose one puppet for each group member.
3. Listen to the song you selected. Make the puppets "sing" with the record.
4. Practice this several times so that puppet mouths are synchronized with the record.
5. Be prepared to have puppets perform for the next Performance Day.

Group Leader: _____

| Group Members: | Helped | Did not Help |
|---|---|---|
|  |  |  |

**Figure 9**

## *The Day of Performance Day*

When the designated Performance Day arrives, the class should sit as an audience, listening to each performing group. The teacher on this day serves as an evaluator, grading each group on: (1) their business-like attitude during performance and (2) the quality of their finished product. Mrs. Dobbs found that the moments immediately following a Performance Day were opportune for a meaningful discussion regarding the work that had just been accomplished. Her students were pleased to have a Performance Day about every two months. And each performing opportunity not only gave additional self-confidence, but also appeared to satisfy the "need to perform" which even the most inhibited seemed to feel.

## TEN IDEAS FOR PERFORMANCE DAY

The following ideas for Performance Day are included in this book because of their simplicity and their proven success. Little or no equipment is required; teacher preparation is relatively easy; and these Performance Day ideas have been effectively used in a wide range of grades.

It is important in developing your plans that you be sure to utilize materials that are familiar to *your* students. If the songs listed here, for example, are unfamiliar, then substitute familiar titles. Always move into new and unfamiliar strategies by utilizing some old and familiar vehicles.

Try a Performance Day in your music classroom. Begin with these ideas; then develop some of your own. As you and your students gain expertise in executing a Performance Day, you will think of other concepts around which student performances may be developed. Think, dream, scheme, borrow, adapt, adopt, and invent!

1. *Writing a Song Parody*

    Equipment needed: paper and pencil

    Directions: Use the tune for one of the following songs and make up some new words (song parody) which would be appropriate for the _____ season. (Fill in Back-to-School, Halloween, Valentine, and so on.) Use no instrumental accompaniment and prepare your *Song Parody* for performance in class.

    Song List:
    1. Rock-a-my-Soul
    2. When the Saints
    3. I've Been Working on the Railroad
    4. _____ (Your Choice)

2. *Making a Song Variation*

    Equipment needed: word sheets for songs on Song List

    Directions: Use one of the following songs and make a *Song Variation* on it. Do not change the words, but do change one of these musical elements: rhythm, tempo, dynamics, mood, or style. Prepare to perform your *Song Variation* as follows:
    a) Announce the musical element which you have changed.
    b) Sing it "straight"
    c) Sing the variation

Song List:
1. Rock-a-my Soul
2. When the Saints
3. I've Been Working on the Railroad
4. Yellow Submarine
5. _____ (Your Choice)

3. *Singing a Song with Instrumental Accompaniment*

Equipment needed: word sheets for songs on Song List; classroom instruments (piano, autoharp, varied percussion)

Directions:
a) Choose a song from the list below.
b) Choose any two instruments to use as accompanying instruments (piano, autoharp, any one of the percussion instruments).
c) Decide which group members will play the instruments.
d) Practice singing your *Song with Instrumental Accompaniment* to perform for the class.

Song List:
1. He's Got the Whole World in His Hands
2. Down by the Riverside
3. Worried Man Blues
4. On Top of Spaghetti
5. Coming Round the Mountain
6. _____ (Your Choice)

4. *Accompanying a Song with Two Different Rhythm Patterns*

Equipment needed: word sheets for songs on Song list; classroom percussion instruments

Directions:
a) Choose any song from the list below.
b) Choose two percussion instruments to accompany the song.
c) Experiment with playing different rhythmic patterns while you sing the song.

d) Decide who will play the instruments for the performance.
e) Prepare to perform your song as follows:
   1) Sing it once with instruments playing a certain rhythm pattern.
   2) Sing it again with instruments playing a *Different Rhythm Pattern*.

Song List:
1. Tom Dooley
2. Home on the Range
3. Worried Man Blues
4. On Top of Spaghetti
5. Down by the Riverside
6. _____(Your Choice)

5. *Creating a Twelve-Tone Row:*
   (Original, Rhythmic Variation, Retrograde, Retrograde Rhythmic Variation)
   
   Equipment needed: one manuscript sheet and pencil per group; twelve resonator bells (one chromatic octave) per group
   
   Directions:
   a) Arrange the twelve tones in any desired order. (Strive for atonality.)
   b) Each group member plays one:
      1) Original
      2) Rhythmic Variation on the Original
      3) Retrograde
      4) Rhythmic Variation on the Retrograde
   c) Choose one person to notate the *Original Twelve-Tone Row*: write names of group members on the paper and file it.

This activity is limited to groups of not more than four.

6. *Making a Sound Piece with Sentences*

   Equipment needed: none

   Directions:
   a) Choose any sentence from the Sentence List below.

    b)  Re-arrange the words of the sentence into any de-
        sired order.

    c)  Using only those words, create a sound piece that
        lasts for about 90 seconds.

        You may use any of these techniques:
           1)  Repeat words.
           2)  "Stretch-out" the sounds.
           3)  Change the pitch of your voice.
           4)  Repeat a single word.
           5)  Use a solo voice with chorus background.
           6)  Use a single syllable to do any of the above.

    d)  Be sure to have your *Sound Piece* well organized.
        (Writing notes to yourself on scrap paper might
        help.)

Sentence List:
    1.  Haste makes waste.
    2.  Give me liberty or give me death.
    3.  Better late than never.
    4.  A stitch in time saves nine.
    5.  The early bird gets the worm.
    6.  A bird in the hand is worth two in the bush.
    7.  _____(Your Choice)

7.  *Creating an Opera*

Equipment needed: none

Directions:
    a)  Choose an opera title from one of these:
           1)  Trouble on the Way to Mars
           2)  No Place to Stay in Chicago
           3)  Donald Duck in Disney World
           4)  A Splendid Soap Opera
           5)  U.F.O. in the U.S.A.
           6)  _____(Your Choice)

    b)  Decide exactly what will happen in your opera. What
        is the story?

    c)  Decide where the scene will take place. What is the
        setting?

d) Decide how many characters are needed for your opera. Who are the characters?

e) Assign a character part to each group member. Somebody may have to take two parts.

f) Decide on the lines each character must say in order to act out the story.

g) Decide on such things as standing, sitting, entering, leaving, walking, and so on. (This is called "blocking.")

h) Practice the play with all "blocking" and with the characters speaking all lines.

i) Decide if props will be needed. If so, get them.

j) Practice the play again, using any necessary props and blocking; this time all lines should be sung. No speaking!

k) Continue practicing until your opera is ready for Performance Day.

8. *Dramatizing a Ballad*

Equipment needed: word sheets or song books that contain songs on Song List

Directions:

a) Choose a ballad from the Song List.

b) Discuss the story of the ballad.

c) Decide which characters are represented in the story.

d) Decide which student will play each character part.

e) Decide how the song will be acted out.

f) Decide how the song will be sung:
   1) solo
   2) group
   3) with a recording

g) Practice your dramatization several times in preparation for Performance Day.

Song List:
1. John Henry
2. Soldier, Soldier, Will You Marry Me?
3. Old Woman, Old Woman
4. Erie Canal
5. Michie Banjo

9. *Creating a Pentatonic Composition*

   Equipment needed: manuscript paper and pencil; diatonic bells or resonator bells to make pentatonic scale (CDEGA)

   Directions:

   a) The group should work together to make one eight-measure composition in 4/4 meter.

   b) Use only the tones of the C pentatonic scale: CDEGA

   c) Use any of the following symbols in your composition:

   $$\circ \quad \phantom{} \quad \text{♩} \quad \text{♪} \quad - \quad \text{𝄾} \quad \text{𝄿} \quad \frown$$

   d) One group member should notate the composition on the manuscript paper.

   e) Practice playing your composition in preparation for the class Performance Day.

10. *Playing, Dancing, or Singing Any Song*

    Equipment needed: as required

    Directions:

    a) Choose any music to sing, play, or dance.

    b) Decide on these:

       1) Will you use an accompaniment? If so, what?
       2) How many verses will you sing?
       3) How many times will you play it?
       4) Do you have a musical leader?
       5) If you choose to dance, do you have the recording?
       6) What about choreography?

    c) Practice your selection in preparation for the class Performance Day.

# 4

## Small Group Activities
## for Project Day

*The best, most beautiful, and most*
*perfect way that we have of expressing*
*a sweet concord of mind to each other*
*is by music.*

Johnathan Edwards

Project Day is a designated day on which small groups of students share their finished projects with the entire class. They choose one project from a list of suggestions and work with other students in developing it. One or more music class periods may be given for working on the projects. Additional time may be spent outside of class, if the group desires.

To facilitate the teacher's "manage-ability" of this small group activity, not more than five different projects should be offered at the same time. To promote creativity among the students, not more than two groups should be permitted to select the same project. Through the use of a sign-up sheet similar to the one shown in Figure 10, students' names may be listed beside their choice of projects. Note that in this activity small groups are formed according to the students' choice of projects. To facilitate this activity, only five projects are listed, with only two groups possible under each heading.

*60*

SIGN-UP SHEET FOR PROJECT DAY

1. Decide which of the suggested projects you want to do.
2. Sign your name under the project chosen.
   (LIMIT: Six people per group)

PROJECT 1: CHOREOGRAPHING A DANCE TO A PIECE OF CLASSICAL MUSIC

Group A: 1 _____ 4_____
         2 _____ 5_____
         3 _____ 6_____

Group B: 1 _____ 4_____
         2 _____ 5_____
         3 _____ 6_____

PROJECT 2: PUPPETS SINGING A SONG

Group A: 1 _____ 4_____
         2 _____ 5_____
         3 _____ 6_____

Group B: 1 _____ 4_____
         2 _____ 5_____
         3 _____ 6_____

PROJECT 3: PRESENTING A PLAY ABOUT A COMPOSER'S LIFE

Group A: 1 _____ 4_____
         2 _____ 5_____
         3 _____ 6_____

Group B: 1 _____ 4_____
         2 _____ 5_____
         3 _____ 6_____

PROJECT 4: DEVELOPING AND PRESENTING A SOUND STORY

Group A: 1 _____ 4_____
         2 _____ 5_____
         3 _____ 6_____

Group B: 1 _____ 4_____
         2 _____ 5_____
         3 _____ 6_____

PROJECT 5: MAKING A MURAL

Group A: 1 _____ 4_____
         2 _____ 5_____
         3 _____ 6_____

Group B: 1 _____ 4_____
         2 _____ 5_____
         3 _____ 6_____

Figure 10

## HOW TO PLAN FOR PROJECT DAY

Planning for Project Day is always affected by such logistical problems as the number of available record players and other equipment. One approach to planning is to make a list of five possible projects, make a rough sketch of the classroom, and then to decide where each of the projects might be best accomplished. Consider the arrangement of your classroom. Take a "mental inventory" regarding the availability of record players, headphones, art supplies, old music books, old professional journals, old music-industry catalogs, puppets, a prop-hat box (containing an assortment of hats, aprons, and scarves), a record cupboard, and a file drawer for student use. In the file drawer place multiple copies of sound stories, plays about composers, and choral readings, all of which may be changed from time to time by adding fresh material and returning others to your personal file.

The consideration of art supplies bears special mention here. Some teachers prefer to supply glue and paper of all types, with the students being held responsible for supplying their own pencils, scissors, crayons, paints, and colored markers. In some schools, there is no problem with permitting a student to return to his locker or homeroom for supplies. In other schools, this could be a problem. Learn to anticipate your own situation.

After pondering and sketching-out the working-sound-level "compatability" of your suggested five projects, as well as checking the availability of all necessary equipment, you should be ready to meet your class. Finally, as the last step in preparing, make ready a sign-up sheet (Figure 10) for each class and two project cards for each suggested project. (A project card is a laminated copy of the suggested project assignment.)

## HOW TO IMPLEMENT PROJECT DAY

If everything has been prepared and carefully planned, implementing Project Day should be a simple task for any music teacher. You may want to begin by listing the five suggested projects on the chalkboard or overhead projector. Announce to the students that they should choose one project from that list and give a quick explanation of what is entailed in each project. Discuss any questions that arise about the projects and ask the students to indicate their choice of project by writing their names on the sign-up sheet. The sign-up sheet may then be posted until Project Day is over.

After all the groups are organized and the projects chosen, each group should be given a project card (containing detailed instructions) to use as a reference during their work on the project. The total time spent in organizing and receiving instructions should be less than ten minutes. Now, with the equipment previously prepared and laid out by the teacher and with the project card in hand, the small groups need only to begin their work. They should know that, as usual, you will evaluate their efforts according to 1) work habits, 2) business-like attitudes toward the project, and 3) quality of the finished project.

The importance of planning ahead for Project Day cannot be over-emphasized, as is illustrated clearly in the case of Miss Fields. She asked her eighth grade music class to choose from a list of five projects—all of which required a record player. Miss Fields did not have five record players, nor did she have electrical outlets to accomodate five record players. Furthermore, she had not stopped to think that a record player would be required for "Creating a Dance," "Singing Puppets," or "Presenting a Poem with Background Music." It was too late when Miss Fields, struggling with chaos and embarrassment, realized that the whole idea was impossible with only her two record players. In desperation, she called the class together and quickly cancelled all of the Project Day assignments until she could work it out more carefully for a future meeting.

Most intermediate grades will enjoy working on a Project Day about two or three times during the school year. You should keep a record indicating the projects chosen so that your students can be guided into choosing different projects each time. All of your project cards (two laminated cards for each suggested project) can be stored in a box for instant availability in the future.

*Suggestion:* Try five projects that all relate to the same topic as an approach to a unit of your choice.

## TEN SUGGESTED PROJECTS FOR PROJECT DAY

These ten projects are given here as a "kick-off" for your students. You will soon want to develop your own ideas, or even those of your students.

1. *Project: Pop Music Dance*

   Equipment needed: Record player
                                Recording

   Procedure:
   1. Choose a "pop" music recording.
   2. Choreograph a dance suitable for it.
   3. Use many contrasting movements.
   4. Be sure that the movements "fit" the music.
   5. Organize the dance carefully.
   6. Practice your dance.
   7. Present the dance to the class.

   *** Perform the dance for another class (optional).

2. *Project: Classical Music Dance*

   Equipment needed: Record player
                                Recording

   Procedure:
   1. Choose a "classical" music recording.
   2. Choreograph a dance suitable for it.
   3. Use many contrasting movements.
   4. Be sure that the movements "fit" the music.
   5. Organize the dance carefully.
   6. Practice your dance.
   7. Present it to the class.

   *** Perform the dance for another class (optional).

3. *Project: Singing Puppets*

   Equipment needed: Record player
                                Recording
                                Puppets with movable mouths
                                Puppet stage

   Procedure:
   1. Choose a recording of any *song*.
   2. Choose hand puppets with movable mouths to pantomime "singing" the recording. Handle the puppets carefully!

3. Move the puppets' mouths in synchronization with each word of the song.
4. Use one puppet when the singing is a solo.
5. Use several puppets when the singing is not a solo.
6. Use swaying or "dancing-type" motions during the instrumental interludes.
7. When there is a solo voice with background singers, use the puppets accordingly.
8. Present your Singing Puppets to the class.

*** Present your Singing Puppets to another class (optional).

4. *Project: Presenting a Folk Dance*

Equipment needed: Record player
                  Musical recording with instructions
                      for a variety of folk dances

Procedures:
1. Choose a folk dance from your recording.
2. Learn the folk dance
3. Practice the dance
4. Demonstrate the dance for your class.

*** Demonstrate the dance for another class (optional).

5. *Project: Making a Mural*

Equipment needed: Mural paper
                  Pencils, crayons, colored markers, or
                      paints

Procedures:
1. Choose a subject for your mural from the following:
   • Music Symbols
   • Music in Nature
   • Instruments of the Orchestra
   • American Workers and their Songs
   • Music in Everyday Life
   • Instruments of the "Top Forty"
   • _____(your choice—be sure that it's related to music.)

2. Decide what each group member will draw on the mural.
3. Organize and assign the space on the mural paper.
4. Be sure that each picture is "right-side up."
5. When detail work is finished, fill in any spaces with background color to "bring it all together."
6. Work carefully.
7. Present the mural to the class.

*** Display the mural in a hallway of your school (optional).

6. *Project: A Sound Story*

   Equipment needed: A collection of Sound Story scripts
                     Percussion instruments
                     Cassette tape recorder (optional)

   Procedure:
   1. Choose a Sound Story.
   2. Choose one group member to be the reader.
   3. Decide what to use for the necessary sound effects. Consider musical instruments as well as your surroundings.
   4. Practice carefully.
   5. Present your finished Sound Story to the class.

   *** Record your Sound Story using a cassette recorder (optional).

7. *Project: Making a Music Game*

   Equipment needed: Miscellaneous art supplies (glue, paper, scissors, crayons)

   Procedures:
   1. Select a subject for your game:
      • Names of notes (A B C D E F G)
      • Kinds of notes ( 𝅝 𝅗𝅥 𝅘𝅥 𝅘𝅥𝅮 )
      • Names of composers
      • Names of songs
      • Names of instruments

- Reading rhythms
- Reading melodies
- _____ (Your choice)

2. Create a game for no more than six players.
   What skill is involved?
   What is the strategy for your game?
3. Make all necessary game pieces.
4. Play the game.
5. Evaluate the game.
   (Discuss this—do not write it down)
6. Demonstrate the game for your music class.

\*\*\* Package your game and leave it with the music teacher so that others may play it.

8. *Project: Presenting a Play About a Composer's Life*

   Equipment needed: A collection of play scripts
   
   Prop-hat box filled with hats, aprons, scarves (optional).

   Procedure:
   1. Choose a play about a composer from the collection provided.
   2. Ass'gn the parts.
   3. Plan where each character will sit, stand, enter, leave, move, and so on.
   4. Plan the props that will be needed.
   5. Practice carefully.
   6. Present the play to the class.

   \*\*\* Present the play to another class (optional).

9. *Project: Making a Music Picture Book for Young Children*

   Equipment needed: Art supplies
   
   (colored paper, crayons, scissors, glue, paints, colored markers)
   
   Tag board cut into uniform pieces, depending on size of book desired—
   8″ × 10″ or 12″ × 15″

Old music books, sheet music, professional magazines, or industry
catalogues.
Paper hole-punch
Yarn

Procedure:

1. Decide which of the following books you will make:
   - Music Symbol Picture Book
     Each page shows a drawing of a music sym-
     bol and the words, "This is a quarter note"
     (or whatever).
   - Composer Picture Book
     Each page shows a picture of a composer
     with the words, "This is Charles Ives" ( or
     whomever).
   - Musical Instrument Picture Book
     Each page shows a picture of a musical in-
     strument with the words, "This is a violin"
     (or whatever).
   - A Song-Picture Book
     Each page contains a complete song with
     pictures that have been taken from old music
     books.
   - Music Symbol "Feel-It" Book
     Use yarn to shape and glue a music symbol
     for each page. Young children will enjoy
     feeling the shapes, and they learn the sym-
     bols.
   - ____(Design your own book.)
2. Assign each group member to make one or two pages
   for the book.
3. Decide what will appear on each page; discuss this so
   that each page can be different.
4. Make every page colorful!
5. Make a cover for the book—complete with title.
6. Punch holes in each page and put the book together
   with colored yarn.

\*\*\* Share your Music Picture Book with another class or
give it as a gift to a younger friend.

10. *Project: Presenting a Choral Reading with Background Music*

Equipment needed: A selection of Choral Readings
A selection of recordings
(RCA *Adventures in Music* or
RCA *Listening Albums*)
Record player

Procedure:
1. Choose a Choral Reading.
2. Assign any lines that need a solo reader.
3. Organize into two groups, if necessary.
4. Practice the Choral Reading.
   (Don't forget to use expression in your voice!)
5. Perform your Choral Reading for your class.

*** After you have chosen your Choral Reading:
1. Select a recording to use as background music with your Choral Reading.
2. Practice the Choral Reading with the recording.
   Are there any places where the music should be turned louder or softer? If so, appoint someone to control the volume.
3. Decide how the music should end.
   Would it sound better with a fade-out?
   Would it sound better with a louder ending?
   Will the music end before or after the Choral Reading?
4. Practice co-ordinating the Choral Reading with the music.
5. Perform your Choral Reading with music for your class.

*** Perform your Choral Reading for another class (optional).

## RESOURCES FOR MUSIC PROJECT DAY

We recommend that you keep an ever-growing file of such things as the Sound Stories, Plays about Composers, and Choral Readings. We have included a few stories, plays, and readings in this chapter to help you get started. You can find others in the usual places, such as in textbooks and in surprising places like magazine and television advertisements. Collect them from everywhere and be sure to save the ones written by you and your students.

### Beethoven Hears Music in the Trees
#### (A play based on a true incident)

Characters:   Ludwig Beethoven, a boy
              Father Beethoven
              Reader

(Scene:   Ludwig is practicing at the piano. Father Beethoven is sitting in a chair nearby).

Ludwig:   "Oh Father! Can't I stop practicing just this once? It is such a beautiful day. The sun is shining. The birds are singing, and I am so tired of practicing these exercises."

Father:   "No! Ludwig. You must practice and practice. Someday you will be famous, and we will at last be rich. Now, get busy."

Ludwig:   "Very well, Father."

Reader:   So little Ludwig continued with his practice. His father slipped out of the room, and Ludwig kept practicing. By and by Ludwig began to get restless again. The birds passed by his window, inviting him to come outside and join them in the beautiful out-of-doors. Ludwig could stand it no longer. He noticed that his father had left him alone. Quickly he climbed off the piano bench and went out the door. He sat down by a big tree. He watched the birds, the forest, and the meadows. He was so happy.

He sat very quietly enjoying all of nature. But inside his head many thoughts were spinning. Let's listen as he thinks aloud.

Ludwig:   "What a beautiful day. What a soft, gentle breeze. The river and the forest seem so big and great. Just listen to the breeze growing stronger and then dying away. Now, listen! The trees! The trees seem to be singing! Singing with the rise and fall of the breeze like a hundred violins! Now the grass seems to be joining in the melody—like flutes. And the waves are lapping and splashing at the river bank. What beautiful music all of it makes together! It's like a magic spell! (He listens quietly for a moment.)

Father: "Ludwig! Ludwig! Come here this instant!"

Ludwig: "Oh, Father, did you hear? Did you hear the beautiful music? The birds, the river, the trees, even the grass were all singing together in a beautiful glorious sound. Someday I am going to write music like that."

Father: "Music in the trees, humph! Next you will be hearing music in the walls of the house. Come, you lazy boy. Get back to your practice."

Ludwig: "Oh, let me just listen a little longer."

Father: "Come at once! You have wasted enough time with this silliness."

Reader: Ludwig returned home with his father. He knew that someday he would again visit nature and write down the beautiful things she whispered in his ear. He knew that he would combine all the sounds into a beautiful symphony for everyone to hear. And he did.

\* \* \*

*George Frederick Handel and His Stubborn Dad*

(A play based on a true incident)

Characters: Narrator
Father Handel
Mother Handel
George Handel, the son
Duke, a rich man

(Scene One: Outside the Handel home, Father Handel is pacing back and forth. Narrator stands at side of the stage area.)

Father: (Angrily stamping his foot) "No! My boy shall never be a musician. He is to be a lawyer."

(Scene Two: Attic of the Handel home. Mother Handel and George are talking.)

Narrator:    One day after that, George Handel's mother gave him a very special birthday present.

Mother:    "Look George, this harpsichord is for you. But we must keep it hidden here in the attic so that your father won't know."

George:    "Oh, what a wonderful present! Thank you. Thank you!"

Mother:    "Let's be very careful to keep our secret from your father. He would be very angry, you know."

George:    "Yes, Mother. I will be very careful. Just think, my very own harpsichord." (George sits at harpsichord and begins to play. Mother Handel leaves him.)

Father:    (off-stage) "George! George!" (Pause. George continues to play.) "George! George, where are you?"

(Pause. George continues to play. Suddenly Father Handel bursts into the room.)

Father:    "George! So here you are. And what is this going on here? I shall take this instrument and destroy it!"

George:    "Oh, please, father. Don't take it away. Please let me keep my birthday present."

Father:    "Well then, play the thing. But remember, someday you are to be a lawyer."

*          *          *

(Scene three:    Inside the Duke's castle. George is sitting at the harpsichord. Father Handel and the Duke are standing outside the door.)

Narrator:    Later, when George was seven years old, his father took him on a visit to the castle of the Duke. While Father Handel and the Duke were talking, they heard great music from the nearby chapel.

Duke:    "That music is beautiful, let us see who is playing!"

(They rush into the chapel)

Duke:    "Why, it is just a boy."

Father:    "It is my stupid son."

Duke: "You must not speak so. A musical talent such as this is rare. You must find the best teacher for the boy."

Narrator: Father Handel was stubborn. He argued with the Duke. But when Father Handel and George returned home from their visit with the Duke, they found a music teacher for George. George was so happy. He could study and write music to his heart's content. His father became happier too. Even though his son was not a lawyer, he knew his son was happy. And the music of George Frederick Handel has made many people happy for more than 200 years.

\* \* \*

### *Franz Joseph Haydn Meets the Empress*

(A play based on a true incident)

Characters: Reader
Joseph, a small boy
Richard, his friend
Paul, another friend
Choirmaster, their choir leader
Empress, a great lady
Nobleman, a friend of the Empress

(Scene One: Inside the palace of the Empress. Scaffolding has been set up for the painters. (Use chairs and tables for the scaffolding.) Reader stands at one side of the stage area.)

Reader: Franz Joseph Haydn, as a lad, was a member of St. Stephen's Boys' Choir in Vienna. Many times his love of fun helped to ease the pains of hunger and homesickness which the choir boys often felt. Once the choir went to sing at the Palace for the great Empress. The choirmaster went out to greet the Empress while the choir boys waited in the assembly room.

Joseph: "Wow! Look at that high scaffolding! Looks like a lot of work going on in here!"

Richard "I'll say! Guess they are going to paint or something."

Joseph: "Sure would be fun to climb upon that high scaffold, eh?"

Paul: "Sure, Joseph. But remember what the choirmaster said, 'Do not go near the scaffolding.' "

Joseph:    "Shucks! I'll bet he stays in there to chat with the Empress
           for at least fifteen more minutes. Come on fellows! (Joseph
           leads the boys as they climb on scaffolding.)

(Empress and Choirmaster enter)

Empress:   "I can hardly wait to hear the little angels sing again."

Choirmaster:   "Yes, dear Empress. Sometimes I, too, think that the
           boys sing like an angel choir. . . Why, where are the
           boys? I gave strict orders for them to be robed and in
           position immediately! Where have they gone?"

(Choirmaster and Empress look all around)

Empress:   (excitedly pointing) "There they are!" (very disgusted now)
           "And I want them to get down from there this minute! Who
           is that up on the highest scaffolding? Bring him right to me."
           (The choirmaster gets the boys down quickly and roughly
           brings Haydn to the Empress.)

Choirmaster:   "Here is the leader of this piece of mischief, your
           Highness."

Empress:   "What is your name, young man?"

Joseph:    (in a little voice) "Franz Joseph Haydn, your Majesty."

Empress:   "Well, I am commanding your choirmaster to see that you
           get a good tanning for this misbehavior!"

Choirmaster:   "Yes Ma'm!!!" (Roughly leads Haydn off stage.
           Other boys follow.)

Empress:   "Humph." (leaves stage)

Reader:    "You can bet that *that* command of the Empress was well
           attended to. Poor Haydn!"

                        *        *        *

(Scene two:   Empress is seated facing the audience)

Reader:    Many years later, the little fun-loving Haydn became Papa
           Haydn, one of the best-loved composers of all of Austria. One
           day, one of his noble friends presented him to the Empress.

Nobleman:   "Dear Empress. I am happy to present to you the best-loved composer in Austria, Franz Joseph Haydn."

(Haydn bows before her.)

Haydn:   "This is a pleasure for me, your Majesty."

Empress:   "And for me, Mr. Haydn. Many times I have enjoyed hearing your music."

Haydn:   "Do you recall the first time you met me, dear Empress? I was high on a scaffold in the palace. For punishment, you ordered a severe tanning. Believe me, it was really severe!"

Empress:   (laughing) "Well, the tanning must have done a great deal of good. Because you have certainly become one of the finest composers that Austria—and indeed, the world—has ever known."

Reader:   It is true. Haydn was then, and still remains, one of the greatest composers the world has ever known.

*   *   *

## Mozart, the Wonder Child
### (A play based on a true incident)

Characters:   Father Mozart
Mother Mozart
Wolfgang Mozart, about four years old
Nannerl, Wolfgang's sister, about seven years old
Narrator

Props Needed:   Recording of Mozart music for piano or harpsichord and record player. You will also need someone to operate the record player.

(Scene:   Inside the Mozart home. Father Mozart is giving a harpsichord lesson to Nannerl. Wolfgang is watching. Narrator stands at side of the stage.)

Wolfgang:   "I want to play, too! Let me play! I can play that piece."

Father:   "Hush, little one. Your little fingers are too short, and the keys

of the harpsichord are stiff and wide. Perhaps I will give you
music lessons next year, but not now. You are too young.''

Narrator:     Finally, to satisfy the little boy, Father Mozart lifted him
              onto the bench. The boy began to move his fingers over the
              keys. Music filled the room. (Pause for recording of harp-
              sichord to create the effect.) Mother rushed in from the
              kitchen to listen. Nannerl and Father watched with great
              surprise. For the little lad could indeed play. In fact, he
              played one of his sister's difficult pieces without missing a
              note!

Father:       "How is this possible?"

Wolfgang:     "Oh, I just remembered it."

Mother        "Such beautiful music from such a tiny little fellow. What do
              you suppose we should do now, Papa?"

Father:       "Our little son is going to be a great musician. We must help
              him to learn all he can. He has been blessed with a great
              gift—and some day the whole world shall know his name!''

Narrator:     So began Wolfgang Mozart's first music lessions. Once he
              heard a piece of music he could play the music note for note.
              This is the amazing story of a small boy who became known
              as "The Wonder Child" in all the royal courts of Europe.
              Today the whole world knows his name.

                          *        *        *

              *John Phillip Sousa and the Borrowed Shirt*
                       (A play based on a true incident)

Characters:   Phillip Sousa, a boy of about ten
              Four boys, his friends
              Mother Sousa
              Mr. Esputa, the violin teacher
              Reader

Props Needed:  a man-size shirt
               violin and bow

(Scene One:   On the playground. Phillip is walking alone talking to
              himself.)

Phillip:     (talking to himself) "I'll be glad when the concert is over tonight. I always get so nervous before I have to play in a concert. I enjoy it all right, but I just get so worried."

First Boy:   "Hey Phillip! Did you forget the game?"

Second Boy:  "We're waiting for you. Come on."

Third Boy:   "You're the best pitcher, you know. And this is our toughest game of the year. Hurry!"

Phillip:     "What? Yes, I guess I did forget. I'm sorry. I can't play today. The orchestra is giving a concert tonight, and I'm the soloist. I have to get home early. Mr. Esputa is counting on me."

Fourth Boy:  "You can't let us down. The game won't last too long. Come on and pitch for us, Phillip. You can still make it to your concert."

Phillip:     "Well, all right."

*          *          *

Reader:      So the boys went happily off to the baseball game. And a tough game it was, too! Phillip pitched his best, but at the end of the ninth inning, the score was tied and the game had to go into an extra inning. The boys were tired. Phillip's team won the game by a single point. The boys shouted with joy and slapped Phillip on the back in congratulations. Suddenly, Phillip remembered the concert and ran home.

(Scene Two:   Inside the Sousa home. Mrs. Sousa is lying down. Phillip runs in.)

Phillip:     "Oh, Mother, I was playing the baseball game and lost track of the time, and now I'm almost late for Mr. Esputa's concert. I really must hurry. But why are you lying down?"

Mother:      "Son, I have a terrible sick headache. I can't get up. Your father has been called out of town, and the younger children are out in the kitchen finding their own supper. I'm sorry I can't go to your concert. Hurry and do your best."

Reader:      Phillip quickly put on his best slacks, new shoes, and clean socks. But when he looked for a clean white shirt, he couldn't find one.

Phillip:     "Oh, what am I to do? I can't disturb Mother. I guess I'll just
             go on to the concert and tell Mr. Esputa about my problem."
             (Phillip leaves)

(Scene Three:   On the stage of the concert hall. Phillip comes running
                in.)

Phillip:     "Oh, Mr. Esputa. I have a problem. I played baseball too late
             and my mother is sick and my father is away and I can't find a
             clean white shirt to wear and I don't know what to do!"

Mr. Esputa:  "Oh, Phillip. Whatever am I going to do with you? Well,
             you know my wife is still at home. Run over there and tell
             her to give you one of my shirts. And hurry! The concert
             begins in ten minutes." (Phillip leaves and puts on the
             large shirt.)

                          *        *        *

Reader:      Phillip did as he was told. Mrs. Esputa helped him get dressed
             in her husband's shirt. It was much too big, but she tucked it
             into his pants and pinned tucks into the sleeves. Just as the
             concert was to begin, Phillip came rushing in. (Phillip enters
             and pantomimes all that the reader says.) He picked up his
             violin and bow. He took his place in front of the orchestra to
             play his solo. He loved playing music, and as he was playing
             he forgot all about his over-size shirt. But then a pin began to
             prick him. Soon another pin pricked him. He squirmed and
             squirmed. His shirttail began coming out of his slacks. He
             kept right on playing, but the audience and the orchestra were
             laughing. At the end of the solo, the audience clapped and
             clapped, but Phillip was very embarrassed. He left the stage,
             laid down his instrument, and covered his face with his hands.
             Mr. Esputa came to him.

Mr. Esputa:  "You played very well, Phillip. Maybe next time you
             will remember not to play baseball so long and to get
             yourself ready for the concert."

Phillip:     "Yes, Mr. Esputa. I think I learned my lesson today."

Reader:      John Phillip Sousa grew up to be a famous musician, but he
             never forgot the concert where he wore the borrowed shirt.

*     *     *

### The Brave Young Indian
(a sound story)

Directions:    Choose a reader. Make an appropriate sound effect after each sentence.

Many moons ago, in the land of the Plains Indian there was trouble.

The Chief called a conference of all of the men of the village.

They gathered around the fire and discussed the problem until the fire dwindled to ashes.

Finally, a young man stood up and volunteered to ride far off to find deer meat for the village.

Early the next morning the young man mounted his pony and rode off into the North Wind.

The young man and the pony rode on and on, getting weaker and weaker.

Finally, they came upon a small water hole where there were two deer drinking.

The young man aimed his bow and arrow and let fly two direct hits.

When the young man returned home with the deer, there was great rejoicing in the village.

### Charlie and Spot in the Forest
(a sound story)

Directions:    Choose a reader. Make an appropriate sound effect after each sentence.

Charlie lived with his family and his dog, Spot, near a big rain forest.

One day Charlie and his dog decided to go exploring in the rain forest.

Charlie ran to a big tree where he tied a large rope.

Then Charlie and Spot held onto the end of the rope and went creeping among the giant plants of the forest.

They came upon a cave which they had never seen before.

Charlie and Spot went into the cave, although they were very frightened by the eerie noise which they heard.

Still holding onto the rope, they came gratefully out of the cave into a pouring rain.

With the help of the rope they were able to find the way home, even though the storm was terrific.

Charlie was glad to be home again with his family and his dog Spot.

## A Ghostly Story
### (a sound story)

Directions:   Choose a reader. Make an appropriate sound effect after each sentence.

On a dark and windy night a stagecoach rumbled along a country road.

In it a timid young girl bounced up and down on the hard cushions.

Suddenly the coach stopped and in stepped an old, old woman.

She was carrying a large black cat.

The old woman stretched a bony hand to the timid young girl.

At that moment the door was thrown violently open and in rushed a tall man wearing a long raincoat.

He stared at the old woman with his two startling eyes.

With a shriek the old woman sprang to the door.

The large black cat gave a howl.

The young girl fainted.

And the tall man disappeared.

## The Unlikely Rocket Trip
### (a sound story)

Directions:   Choose a reader. Make an appropriate sound effect after each sentence.

The astronauts went into their rocket ship.

They checked the radio, which was filled with static.

They fired the rockets to make the ship leave the ground.

As they reached outer space they heard a strange noise on the hull of their rocket ship.

They looked and saw a hyena which was hanging on for dear life.

The poor hyena had jumped onto their rocket ship when they had passed by a forest on their way up.

A shooting star came zooming by and startled the hyena and the astronauts.

The astronauts slowly let the rocket ship down for a landing.

When it touched, they climbed out to rescue the hyena.

The hyena and the astronauts became the most famous people of the year.

And they got their pictures in all of the newspapers.

### The Walk Home from School
#### (a sound story)

Directions:   Choose a reader. Make an appropriate sound effect after each sentence.

As Marty neared home he was drawing farther and farther from the noise of the highway.

The noise of the trucks was fading away.

The squeal of the brakes was fading away.

Soon the only thing he heard was the twitter of birds.

As Marty walked slowly toward his home, the footpath seemed to crackle pleasantly with each step.

Marty could hear his heart beating with the joy of being alone on the country road.

He heard the rhythm of his horse, Smokey, running in the meadow.

He heard the bouncing of a rubber ball, and he knew his little brother was near.

He knew that his mom would be in the kitchen making familiar cooking noises.

And Marty felt so happy and contented that it seemed his heart would burst with joy!

*I Hear America Singing*

Walt Whitman

(a choral reading)

| | |
|---|---|
| All: | I hear America Singing,<br>the varied carols I hear; |
| Solo: | Those of mechanics—each one singing his, as it should be, blithe and strong; |
| Solo: | The carpenter singing his, as he measures his plank or beam, |
| Solo: | The mason singing his, as he makes ready for work, or leaves off work; |
| Solo: | The boatman singing what belongs to his in his boat —the deck-hand singing on the steamboat deck; |
| Solo: | The shoemaker singing as he sits on his bench—the hatter singing as he stands; |
| Solo: | The wood-cutter's song—the ploughboy's, on his way in the morning, or at noon intermission, or at sundown; |
| Solo: | The delicious singing of the mother—or of the young wife at work—or of the girl sewing or washing— |
| All: | Each singing what belongs to him or her, and to none else; |
| Group A: | The day what belongs to the day— |
| Group B: | At night, the party of young fellows, robust, friendly. |
| All: | Singing, with open mouths, their strong melodious songs. |

### Leave Her, Johnny, Leave Her
Traditional
(a choral reading)

Solo:   I thought I heard the old man say,

All:   Leave her, Johnny, leave her!

Solo:   You can go ashore and draw your pay,

All:   It's time for us to leave her.

Solo:   Oh the times are hard and the wages low,

All:   Leave her, Johnny, leave her!

Solo:   I'll pack my bag and go below,

All:   It's time for us to leave her.

Solo:   It's growl you may, but go you must,

All:   Leave her, Johnny, leave her!

Solo:   It matters not whether you're last or first,

All:   It's time for us to leave her.

Solo:   I'm getting thin and growing sad,

All:   Leave her, Johnny, leave her!

Solo:   Since first I joined this wooden-clad,

All:   It's time for us to leave her.

Solo:   I thought I heard the first mate say,

All:   Leave her, Johnny, leave her!

Solo:   Just one more drag and then belay!

All:   It's time for us to leave her.

### Lady and Swine
Traditional
(a choral reading)

All:   There was a lady loved a swine,

Girls:   "Honey," quoth she,
"Pig-hog, wilt thou be mine?"

Boys:   "Humph," quoth he.

Girls:   "I'll build thee a silver sty,
         Honey," quoth she.
         "And in it thou shall lie,"

Boys:    "Humph," quoth he.

Girls:   "Pinned with a silver pin,
         Honey," quoth she.
         "That thou mayest go out and in."

Boys:    "Humph," quoth he.

Girls:   "Will thou now have me,
         Honey," quoth she.

Boys:    "Humph, humph, humph," quoth he,

All:     And went his way.

## Mystic Night
### Grace Rowe
### (a choral reading)

Group A:   This is the night when the black cats prowl;

Group B:   This is the night when the black cats yowl:

All:       Me-ow!  Me-ow-ow!  Pst!  Pst!

Group A:   This is the night when the brownies prance;

Group B:   This is the night when the brownies dance:

All:       Tip-tippy-tip!  Tip-tippy-toe!

Group A:   This is the night when the goblins moan;

Group B:   This is the night when the goblins groan:

All:       Yow-oo!  Yow-oo!  Yow-oo-oo-oo!

Group A:   The is the night when the witches brew;

Group B:   This is the night when the witches stew:

All:       Mumble-dee-dee!  Mumble-dee-do!

Group A:   This is the night when the winds blow ill;

Group B:   This is the night when the winds blow shrill:

All:       Whoo-oo!  Whoo-oo!  Who-oo-oo!

| | |
|---|---|
| Group A: | This is the night when the lanterns leer; |
| Group B: | This is the night when the lanterns jeer: |
| All: | He-he-he!  Ha-ha-ha!  Ho-ho! |
| Group A: | This is the mystic night of the year; |
| Group B: | This is the mystic night we all fear: |
| All: | Pst!!  Me-ow!!  Who-oo-oo!! |

*Jazz Fantasia*
Carl Sandburg
(a choral reading)

| | |
|---|---|
| All: | Drum on your drums, batter on your banjoes, sob on your long cool winding saxophones, |
| | Go to it, O jazzmen! |
| | Sling your knuckles on the bottoms of the happy tin pans; |
| | Let your trombones ooze, and go hush-a-hush-a-hush on the slippery sand paper. |
| Solo: | Moan like an autumn wind high in the lonesome tree-tops; |
| Solo: | Moan soft like you wanted somebody terrible. |
| Solo: | Cry like a racing car slipping away from a motorcycle cop! |
| Group A: | Bang, bang, you jazzmen! Band all together, drums, traps, banjoes, horns, tin-cans! |
| Group B: | Make two people fight on the top of a stairway and scratch each other's eyes in a clinch tumbling down the stairs. |
| | Can the rough stuff! |
| Solo: | Now a Mississippi steamboat pushes up the night river, with a hoo-hoo-hoo, |
| Solo: | And the green lanterns calling to the high soft stars; |
| Solo: | A red moon rides on the humps of the low river hills; |
| All: | Go to it, O jazzmen! |

### There Will Come Soft Rains
Sara Teasdale
(a choral reading)

Group A:      There will come soft rains and the smell of the ground,
And swallows circling with their shimmering sound;

Group B.      And frogs in the pools singing at night,
And wild plum trees in tremulous white;

Group C:      Robins will wear their feathery fire,
Whistling their shims on a low fence-wire;

All:            And not one will know of the war, not one
Will care at last when it is done.

Not one would mind, neither bird nor tree,
If mankind perished utterly;

And Spring herself, when she woke at dawn,
Would scarcely know that we were gone.

# 5

## Procedures and Activities for Rotation Day

*Whoever has skill in music is of good temperament and fitted for all things.*

Martin Luther

Rotation Day uses five to eight different learning stations where student groups may work for an assigned number of minutes; then they "rotate" to the next learning station for the same number of minutes and so on. Rotation Day may actually span three or more music class meetings.

The prepared learning stations may offer a great variety of musical experiences, such as:

- investigating the work of a certain composer.
- hearing and analyzing a musical composition,
- playing a musical game
- practicing instruments such as resonator bells, ukuleles, autoharps, and recorders.

The scope of activities that may be incorporated into Rotation Day learning stations is limited only by your resourcefulness. Taking the time to plan a Rotation Day experience for your music class will be a rewarding experience for you and your students.

## HOW TO PLAN FOR ROTATION DAY

In planning for Rotation Day, consideration of such factors as electrical outlets and availability of record players/headphones is, again, of critical importance. In preparing for six learning stations, we recommend that only two require record players. If you are the kind of music teacher who is constantly seeking ways for students to learn more music literature and to become critical music listeners, you may choose to set up a "Pop Music Station" and a "Classical Music Station."

A "Pop Music Station" and a "Classical Music Station" are "headphone activities"—both relatively quiet. A "Composer Station" also will involve quiet work. Taking into consideration the working-sound-level of the total class, some music teachers prefer to place the non-quiet learning stations (bells, recorders, music games) between the quiet ones. This system of strategically placing the quiet stations (pop music, classical musical, and composers) between the non-quiet stations offers further contrast when written worksheets are used in the quiet stations. The point is to be sure to consider the working-sound-level of each station as you plan and organize a Rotation Day.

One successful formula for developing a music class Rotation Day is this: Prepare six learning stations that include three quiet stations and three non-quiet stations, all of which offer the student a contrast in scope and type of activity. Within the framework of this formula, many different successful learning experiences may be provided for your students.

## HOW TO IMPLEMENT ROTATION DAY

In introducing the music class to the Rotation Day experience, the music teacher should take the time to demonstrate, or have students demonstrate, the activity that takes place at each station. Students should have a *thorough* understanding of each station and what they are expected to do. To emphasize this further, complete written directions should be posted at each station. After all of the learning stations have been discussed and/or demonstrated, the students should be organized into small groups (four or six per group), and the number of student groups should equal the number of learning stations. For example, if there are six learning stations, there should be six groups. Each group is given a Rotation Day Checklist (Figure 11); and each group is assigned to one of the prepared learning stations. At the end of the previously announced time limit, lights may be blinked as a signal or you may quietly move among the groups advising them to move to the next

---

ROTATION DAY CHECK-LIST FOR STUDENT GROUPS

Captain _____

Recorder_____

Equipment Manager _____

Clean-up Manager _____

Observer _____

File Clerk _____

In the space below, the Recorder should write:
1. The name of the Learning Station
2. The date on which your group worked at that station.
3. Your rating of your group's work. (Excellent, Good, or Fair)

| Name of Learning Station | Date | Rating | | |
| --- | --- | --- | --- | --- |
| | | Excellent | Good | Fair |
| 1. | | | | |
| 2. | | | | |
| 3. | | | | |
| 4. | | | | |
| 5. | | | | |
| 6. | | | | |

**Figure 11**

station. Point out that since a time limit (we suggest ten or fifteen minutes) will be imposed at each station, some students may finish the assigned task early and others may not finish at all. Students who finish quickly should be advised to help the slower ones; and students who fail to finish should be assured that completion will not be a point of assessment. Students also should be cautioned against wandering away from the assigned station.

When Mr. Carpenter decided to implement Rotation Day in his music class, he was apprehensive. His students had, in the past, been negative and unresponsive to many things. But he carefully prepared six different learning stations in his classroom, planning thoroughly and considering factors such as working-sound-level, equipment, and space. He found the results to be amply rewarding. The students were pleased with the variety of activities, the change of pace, and the "new look" in their music room. Mr. Carpenter's apprehension changed to pleasure, especially when he realized that the Rotation Day would consume three full periods of music class. Careful planning had given him several days to serve as observer and advisor in the music class. He considered that aspect to be one of the chief attributes of Rotation Day. He considered it very important that the students be required to work independently and in student-controlled situations from time to time.

## Evaluation

Assessment should be accomplished by the teacher on the basis of the students' ability to 1) follow directions, 2) use good work habits, and 3) give accurate responses to written worksheets. Upon the completion of a Rotation Day experience, each student will have several written worksheets to take home. Such "take-homes" are important, from time to time, in keeping the community aware of the school's music education program.

## How to Save Time with Preparations

Rotation Day is a type of music class experience that requires a lot of advance thought and preparation on your part. The marking of papers and recording of scores may also require much teacher time. By using ideas similar to ones found in "How to Organize Student Evaluation to Prevent the Paper Monster" in Chapter 2, you can save much time. During the three or so days when the class is actually working at the learning stations, the music teacher may find that the class functions very well with little or no teacher input. The pleasure of seeing this happen to a class has caused many music teachers to decide that Rotation Day is definitely worth the "extra effort." And, like Project Day, once it has been accomplished, the teacher already has a head-start in planning for the next Rotation Day. Your students will be happy to have Rotation Day as often as you can manage it. Once every two months seems to be a realistic objective.

An example of a "To-Do List for Rotation Day Success" is:

1. Is each learning station complete with all necessary equipment? (This is extremely important!)
2. Are instructions posted at each station?
3. Is the name of each station posted beside it?
4. Are the Rotation-Day checklists (Figure 11) ready for each student group?
5. Is there one folder for each class in which the groups may file their checklists from day to day?
6. Do the stations offer a variety of learning experiences?

## IDEAS FOR ROTATION DAY

You can develop your own ideas for Rotation Day by simply isolating an area (concept, subject, skill, competency) that you want your students to reinforce. When you have isolated the topic for study, develop the instructional strategy you wish to use. You may decide to use a worksheet, a task card, or perhaps a game.

To help you get started this chapter includes ideas for worksheets (pop music, classical music, famous performers, famous composers, musical instruments) and task cards (diatonic bells, autoharp, piano, recorder). Also included are directions for seven new music games.

A variation on Rotation Day is Action Day. Complete directions for Action Day are given at the end of this chapter.

### Five Ideas with Student Worksheet

1. *Pop Music Listening Station*

    Equipment needed: Record player and six headphones
    Designated record (currently popular)

> Worksheet/pencil for each group
> member
> File folder for completed worksheets
> (one per class)
> Box for file folders (one only)

Activity:
> Each individual student should complete the work-
> sheet while listening to the recording. Several hear-
> ings are recommended. Upon completion, the work-
> sheet should be placed in the file folder provided.
> After making some individual effort, the group mem-
> bers may help each other in completing the worksheet
> (Figure 12).

Suggestion:   Repeat this activity another day, using a dif-
> ferent recording.

2. *Classical Music Listening Station*

Equipment needed: Record player and six headphones
> Designated record
> Worksheet/pencil for each group
> member (Figure 12)
> File folder for completed worksheets
> (one per class)
> Box for file folders (one only)

Activity:
> Each individual student should complete the work-
> sheet while listening to the recording. Several hear-
> ings are recommended. Upon completion, the work-
> sheet should be placed in the file folder provided.
> After making some individual effort, the group mem-
> bers may help each other in completing the worksheet.

Suggested musical selections:
> *Stars and Stripes Forever* (Sousa)
> "Polka" from *Golden Age* (Shostakovitch)
> "Little Fugue in G Minor" (Bach)
> Third Movement, Violin Concerto in D Major
> (Beethoven)
> "Romanze"—*Eine Kleine Nachtmusic* (Mozart)

Student's Name_____
Grade/Homeroom_____

Circle the appropriate title:

POP MUSIC LISTENING STATION

CLASSICAL MUSIC LISTENING STATION

Write the answers in the blank provided.

You may need to listen to the recording several times.

Do your own work; but if you need help, ask another member of your group for help.

Name of musical selection: _____

Name of composer: _____

Name of recording artist: _____

1. _____ Is there an introduction? (yes or no)
2. _____ Name the first instrument (or group of instruments) that you hear in this compostion.
3. _____ Does the music have a "main theme section"? (yes or no)
4. _____ Is the composition performed by a soloist? (yes or no)
5. _____ Does this selection have a constant beat that never changes? (yes or no)
6. _____ Name the instrument which is heard most often in the entire recording.
7. _____ Is the music in a major key or a minor key?
8. _____ Is the music in duple meter or triple meter?
9. List all of the instruments that you hear in this recording.
10. In your own words, write what you think is the mood and meaning of this musical composition.

**Figure 12**

> *Prince of Denmark March* (Clarke)
> *The Moldau* (Smetana)
> *Little Train of Caiperia* (Villa-Lobos)

Suggestion:    Repeat this activity another day, using a different recording.

3.  *Music Performers' Station*

Equipment needed: Vertical file containing books, magazines, and clippings about present-day music performers.
Worksheet/pencil for each group member (Figure 13)
File folder for completed worksheets (one per class)
Box for file folders (one only)

Activity:
The teacher indicates which music performer is being studied, and each individual student should complete the worksheet by using the available resource material. Upon completion, the worksheets should be placed in the file folder provided. After making some individual effort, the group members may help each other in completing the worksheet.

Suggestion:    Repeat this activity another day, assigning a different music performer.

4.  *Composers' Station*

Equipment needed: Reference books or materials and/or filmstrips with viewer
Worksheet/pencil for each group member (Figure 14)
File folder for completed worksheets (one per class)
Box for file folders (one only)

Activity:
The teacher indicates the composer for study, and each individual student uses the reference books or

---

Student's Name_____
Grade/Homeroom_____

## FAMOUS PERFORMERS OF MUSIC

Write as many answers as you can find.

Name of performer
1. Date of birth _____
2. Place of birth _____
3. Age at which musical training began _____
4. Where was first musical job? _____
5. What and where was the first musical success? _____
   _____
6. Notable failures along the way _____
7. Married (yes or no) _____
8. Name of spouse _____
9  Number of children _____
10. Where is this artist living today? _____
11. Name of recording company and/or agent _____
12. Most famous success (record or show) _____
13. Anything else? _____
   _____
14. List the titles of the books, magazines, or clippings which
   you used to find the information. _____
   _____
   _____

---

**Figure 13**

materials provided to complete the worksheet. Upon
completion, the worksheets should be placed in the
file folder. After working individually, the group
members may help each other in completing the
worksheet.

Suggestion:  Repeat this activity another day, assigning a
           different composer.

Student's Name _____
Grade/Homeroom _____

## FAMOUS COMPOSERS OF MUSIC

Write in as many answers as you can find.

Name of composer _____

1. Date of birth _____
2. Date of death _____
3. Name of country where composer was born _____
4. Age at which musical training began _____
5. Where did the composer receive his training? _____
6. Age at which musical job began _____
7. What was the first job? _____
8. Where was the first job? _____
9. First successful composition _____
10. Notable failures along the way _____
11. Married (yes or no) _____
12. Name of spouse _____
13. Number of children _____
14. Most famous compositions _____
    _____
15. List any other things that you learned about this composer
    today _____
    _____
16. List the titles and authors of the reference materials you used
    to find this information _____
    _____

**Figure 14**

5. *Instrument Info Station*

   Equipment needed: Several reference books or materials
   concerning musical instruments
   Worksheet/pencil for each student
   (Figure 15)

---

Student's Name _____
Grade/Homeroom _____

## MUSICAL INSTRUMENTS INFO

Name of instrument _____
1. To which family group does the above instrument belong?

   _____
2. What is this instrument made of? _____
3. What produces sound in the instrument? (vibrating strings, vibrating air column, vibrating reed, or other vibrating body)

   _____
4. What is the general range of the instrument? (high sounds or low sounds) _____
5. Is this instrument normally used in a symphony orchestra? (yes or no) _____
6. About when was this instrument first used? _____
7. In what country or civilization was this instrument first used?

   _____
8. Is this instrument commonly used for special sound effects? (yes or no) _____ If "yes" what are they? _____

   _____
9. List any other things that you learned today about this instrument _____

   _____
10. List the titles and authors of the reference materials you used to provide the information given above. _____

   _____

   _____

---

**Figure 15**

File folder for completed worksheets
(one per class)
Box for file folders (one only)

Activity:
The teacher indicates which instrument to study, and

each individual student uses the reference books and materials to complete the worksheet. Upon completion, the worksheets should be placed in the file folder. After working individually, group members may help each other in completing the assignment.

Suggestion: Repeat this activity another day, assigning a different musical instrument.

## *Five Ideas with Task Cards*

### 1. *Diatonic Bell Station*

Equipment needed: Six diatonic bells with mallets
Three sets of diatonic bell task cards
(Figure 16)

Activity:

Each student plays a diatonic bell according to the music given on the diatonic bell task cards. Students should all work on the same card at the same time and strive to play each song together. (The teacher may provide as many cards as desired. The students begin with card #1, and when they are able to perform this tune, they proceed to card #2, and so on. It is recommended that each card be laminated and that they be stored by title in a box labeled "Diatonic Bell Task Cards.")

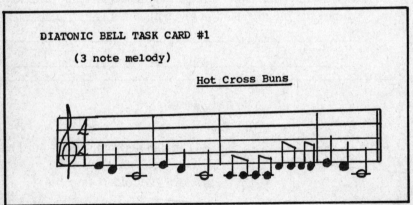

Figure 16

Suggestion:   Repeat this activity another day, assigning the students to work on different diatonic bell task cards.

**Figure 16 (cont'd.)**

**Figure 16 (cont'd.)**

2.  *Autoharp Station*

> Equipment needed: Autoharp and pick for every two group
> members (autoharps should be
> tuned together)
> Three sets of autoharp task cards
> (Figure 17)

Activity:
> Each student plays the autoharp according to assign-
> ment on the autoharp task cards. Students should all
> work on the same cards at the same time and strive to
> play each song together. (The teacher may provide as
> many cards as desired at any level of difficulty. It is
> recommended that each card be laminated and that
> they be stored in a box labeled "Autoharp Task
> Cards.")

> Suggestion:  Repeat this activity another day, assigning
> the students to work on different autoharp
> task cards.

AUTOHARP TASK CARD #1
   (one chord)                        Frère Jacques

F          F              F              F
Frère Jacques, Frère Jacques, dormez-vous, dormez-vous?

Are you sleeping, are you sleeping, Brother John, Brother John?

F                    F
Sonnez les matines, sonnez les matines.

Morning bells are ringing, morning bells are ringing.

F     F   F        F
Din Din Don.  Din Din Don.

Ding Ding Dong.  Ding Ding Dong.

---

**AUTOHARP TASK CARD #2**

   **(two chords)**

                        Lone Star Trail
      F                    F
   Started on the trail on June twenty-third;
         C⁷                        F
   I been punchin' Texas cattle on the Lone Star Trail.
         C⁷                      F
   Singing ki-yi-yip-ee- yip-ee--ay  yip-ee-ay;
   C⁷                          F
   Ki - yi- yip - ee   yip - ee- ay.

---

**AUTOHARP TASK CARD #3**

   **(two chords)**

            Row, Row, Row Your Boat
      C           C
   Row, row, row your boat
      C              C
   Gently down the stream.
      C               C
   Merrily, merrily, merrily, merrily,
      G⁷            C
   Life is but a dream.

**Figure 17**

```
AUTOHARP TASK CARD #4
   (two chords)


                    He's Got The Whole World

          F              F                      F
          He's got the whole world in His hands;
                       C⁷                     C⁷
          He's got the whole world in His hands;
                       F                       F
          He's got the whole world in His hands,
                       C⁷                  C⁷ F
          He's got the whole world in His hands.
```

```
    AUTOHARP TASK CARD #5

       (three chords)



        Michael, Row The Boat Ashore


        C         C          C        F C
        Michael, row the boat ashore, Alleluia.
                  C          G⁷      C G⁷C
        Michael, row the boat ashore, alleluia.
```

```
    AUTOHARP TASK CARD #6

       (three chords)

                       Kum - Bah - Yah
        C          C           F          C
        Kum - bah - yah, my Lord, Kum - bah - yah.
        C          C                      G⁷
        Kum - bah - yah, my Lord, Kum - bah - yah.
        C          C           F          C
        Kum - bah - yah, my Lord, Kum - bah - yah.
        F  C    G⁷        C
        Oh, Lord,  Kum - bah - yah.
```

**Figure 17 (cont'd.)**

3. *Piano Station*

> Equipment needed: Two pianos
>> Two sets of piano task cards (one set for each piano) (Figure 18)

> Activity:
>> Each student plays the piano according to the assignment on the piano task cards. Students should all work on the same task card at the same time. Two or three students may work together at the same piano. Students should strive to play each exercise together. (The teacher may provide as many cards as desired at any level of difficulty. It is recommended that each card be laminated and that they be stored in a box labeled "Piano Task Cards.")

> Suggestion: Repeat this activity another day, assigning the students to work on different piano task cards.

---

PIANO TASK CARD #1
    (Black keys)

Black-Key Boogie

Play the Black-Key Boogie up and down on the black keys of the piano.(Begin on F#)

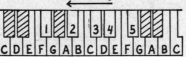

The pattern contains eight sounds.  Count them as you play.

Play the pattern four times.

Stop on the beginning key.

---

**Figure 18**

PIANO TASK CARD #2
      (C scale)

<u>C Major Scale</u>

Play the ascending C Major Scale on the piano

Begin on any "C."

Use any fingering.

Play the scale twice.

PIANO TASK CARD #3
      (G scale)

<u>G Major Scale</u>

Play the ascending G Major Scale on the piano

Begin on any "G."

Use any desired fingerings

Play the scale twice.

PIANO TASK CARD #4
      (F scale)

<u>F Major Scale</u>

Play the ascending F Major Scale on the piano

Begin on any "F."

Any fingering pattern is acceptable.

Play the scale twice.

**Figure 18 (cont'd.)**

PIANO TASK CARD #5
    (C Chord)

<u>C Chord</u>

Play any C Major chord.

Play the chord three times.

---

PIANO TASK CARD #6
    (F Chord)

<u>F  Chord</u>

Play any F Major Chord.

Play the chord three times.

---

PIANO TASK CARD #7
    (G Chord)

<u>G Chord</u>

Play any G Major chord.

Play the chord three times.

**Figure 18 (cont'd.)**

PIANO TASK CARD #8
    (three chords)

I - IV - V
Chords in C Major

Play the following chords in the order given:

C  C  C     F  F  F     G  G  G     C  C  C

---

PIANO TASK CARD #9
    (3 note melody)

Hot Cross Buns

3  2  1  -  3  2  1  -  1 1 1 1 2 2 2 2 3  2  1  -

---

PIANO TASK CARD #10
    (5 note melody)

When The Saints Go Marching In

1 3 4  5    1 3 4  5    1 3 4  5 3 1 3

2      3 2 1 1 3 5  5 4    3 4  5 3 1 2  1

Figure 18 (cont'd.)

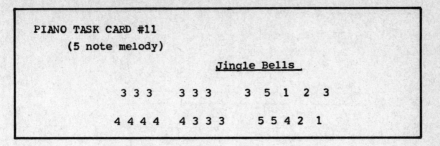

PIANO TASK CARD #11
(5 note melody)

Jingle Bells

3 3 3     3 3 3     3 5 1 2 3

4 4 4 4   4 3 3 3     5 5 4 2 1

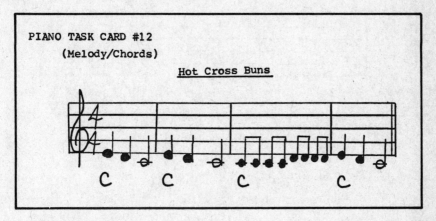

PIANO TASK CARD #12
(Melody/Chords)

Hot Cross Buns

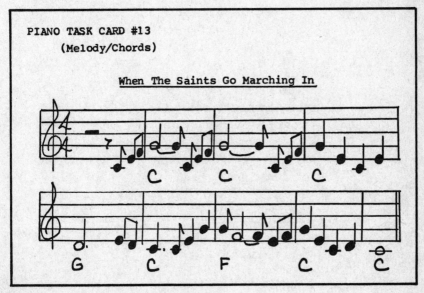

PIANO TASK CARD #13
(Melody/Chords)

When The Saints Go Marching In

Figure 18 (cont'd.)

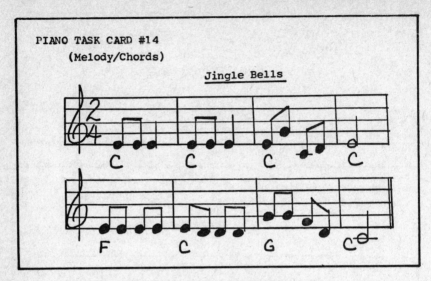

**Figure 18 (cont'd.)**

4. *Recorder Station*

   Equipment needed: Six recorders
                     Fingering charts for recorders
                     Three sets of recorder task cards
                        (Figure 19)
                     Disinfectant spray or solution

   Activity:
       Each student plays a recorder according to the as-
       signment on the recorder task cards. Students should
       all work on the same cards at the same time and strive
       to play each song together. The teacher may provide
       as many cards as desired. It is recommended that each
       card be laminated and that they be stored in a box
       labeled "Recorder Task Cards."

   Suggestion: Repeat this activity another day, assigning
               the students to work on different recorder
               task cards.

5. *Game Station*

   Equipment needed: Game equipment as specified

Activity:

  The teacher may provide any three or four music games at the game station. The students in each group should participate in selecting and playing one or two of the games. Each game should be packaged with complete directions and all necessary equipment. Several games are presented in the following "Music Game Resources" section.

  Suggestion: Repeat this activity another day and provide a different set of games for students to play.

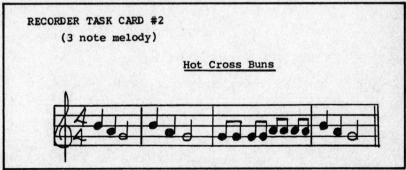

**Figure 19**

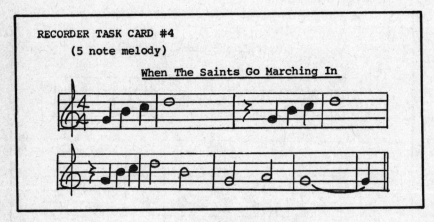

**Figure 19 (cont'd.)**

## *MUSIC GAME RESOURCES*

### *Orchestra Pit*

General Musical Concept:  Musical instruments

Skill Involved:  Recognizing names of instrument families

Recommended Grade Levels:  4-8

Number of Players:  four to six

Equipment needed:  16 playing cards with each card having the name
of one instrument. Among the 16 cards, there

should be four woodwind, four string, four brass, and four percussion instruments.

Directions:

Cards are shuffled and dealt to the players. After players have looked at the cards, the dealer declares "overture." Players trade cards freely until one player has a set of four cards which represent instruments of the same orchestral family. The player who holds the matching set calls "finale," and that round is over. The game continues with a new dealer.

## Musical Perquackey

General Musical Concept:  Naming notes

Skills Involved:    Naming notes of treble or bass clef
                    Forming words

Grade Levels Recommended:  4-8

Number of Players:  Small group

Equipment:  Six small cubes that have been prepared with a staff and one note on each side of each cube. (Be sure that among the six cubes all of the musical alphabet is included.)
One-minute timer (optional)
A closed cylinder to use for a shaker (optional)
Paper/pencil for recording scores

Directions:

The first player rolls all of the cubes. With the letters that turn up, he spells words. At the end of one minute, he records his score and the play passes to the next player.

Scoring system:

1 point for each cube used.
5 points bonus if all cubes are used.
10 points bonus if all cubes are used in a single word.
The highest score determines the winner.

## Rhythm Bowl

General Musical Concept:  Rhythmic notation

Skill Involved:   Adding measures of rhythm

Grade Levels Recommended:   4-8

Number of Players:   Small groups

Equipment:   Six cardboard tubes or other upright objects with a music
symbol displayed on each:

♩. ♩ ♩ 𝅝 ▬ 𝄽

A sponge ball about four inches in diameter.

Directions:

Stand the tubes in a row on the floor. Players are divided into
teams. The teams take turns rolling the ball to knock down the
tubes. Each player may roll as many times as necessary to make
one measure of four beats. If count exceeds what is needed for one
measure, the play passes to the other team. Each correct measure is
worth four points.

### Before the Fall

General Music Concept:   Note names

Skill Involved:   Naming of notes of treble clef

Recommended Grade Levels:   4-8

Number of Players:  Small groups

Equipment:   Large music staff on floor
A set of any kind of treble clef note cards (or bass if you
wish)

Directions:

The players take turns, one at a time, advancing to the floor staff
and then following the directions of the designated "caller." The
caller's job is to randomly select a treble clef note card which he
calls; e.g., "First space F." The player then must place his right
hand on the note called. The caller calls another note, and the
player must place his left hand on it—keeping his right hand where
it is. The third note called is always for the right foot, and the fourth
note called is always for the left foot. The player should always try
to place the feet without moving the hands. If a player is able to
accomplish all four notes without falling, he earns five points. If he

falls, he earns one point for each note accomplished before the fall. The four notes called must always be indicated in this order: right hand, left hand, right foot, left foot.

### Musical Yahtze

**General Musical Concept:** Writing rhythmic notation

**Skill Involved:** Drawing notes and rests

**Grade Levels Recommended:** 4-8

**Number of Players:** Small groups

**Equipment:** A Toss-a-Cube
(This cube has been prepared with one of the following symbols on each side of it.)

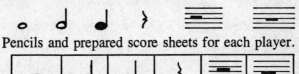

Pencils and prepared score sheets for each player.

**Directions:**
The first player rolls the Toss-a-Cube. The symbol which turns up should be copied on the appropriate square on his score sheet. Play passes to the other player. Play continues in this way, with each player attempting to complete all of the squares on his score sheet. Only one roll of the Toss-a-Cube is allowed in any turn. The first player who completes his score sheet is the winner.

### War-on-Notes

**General Musical Concept:** Rhythmic notation

**Skill Involved:** Recognizing relative values of rhythmic notation

**Grade Levels Recommended:** 4-8

**Number of Players:** Small groups

**Equipment:** A deck of 40 playing cards which have been constructed by drawing each one of the following symbols on 8

cards. The set of 40 cards should have 8 cards that are alike with each of the symbols.

♩    ♩·    ♩    ♩    ♪

Directions:

Shuffle and deal the cards equally to each player. Each player discards one card from his hand. The player who discarded the "highest" card (the greatest note value) then takes all of the cards for himself. Play continues in this way until all cards have been played. In the event of a tie during a round, another round of cards is discarded and the winner takes all. The player with the largest collection of "discards" at the end of the game is the winner.

## Spin a Sonata

General Music Concept:    Sonata Form

Skill Involved:  Ordering the components of Sonata Form

Recommended Grade Levels:  4-8

Number of Players:  Small groups

Equipment:    A game board spinner which has been marked into five equal segments: Introduction, Exposition (or Section A), Development (or Section B), Recapitulation (or Section A), and Coda.

A score sheet for each player.

| | |
|---|---|
| 1.  Introduction | |
| 2.  Exposition (Section A) | |
| 3.  Development (Section B) | |
| 4.  Recapitulation (Section A) | |
| 5.  Coda | |

Directions:

The object of the game is for each player, in turn, to complete his score sheet in the order that it appears on the score sheet (and in Sonata Form). At each turn, each player spins once only. When his spinner indicates "Introduction," he writes that word in the space provided, and then he is ready to try for the word "Exposition," and so on. After each spin, the play passes to the next player. The first player who completes his score card is the winner. Try the same score sheet for listening to a Sonata Form!

## ACTION DAY

### (A Variation on Rotation Day)

Action Day is a free choice of stations, contingent upon availability, with no time limitations. Six or more stations are prepared around the room as for Rotation Day. A large pocket chart is prepared with two pockets provided for each of the prepared stations (Figure 20). Each pair of pockets should be labeled "Available" and "In Use." Six blank tickets should be placed in each of the "Available" pockets. (Suggestion: Use a different color for each station.) The students, in designated order, select the station in which they desire to work, remove one card from the "Available" pocket, and place it in the appropriate "In Use" pocket. When a station has been chosen by six students, it is automatically closed to others. Work proceeds at the chosen stations until tasks are completed. Upon completion of a station's assigned task, the student may choose to work at another station if a place is available.

# ACTION DAY

Stations Available                                    Stations in Use

|                    |   POP MUSIC        |                    |

|                    |   CLASSICAL MUSIC  |                    |

|                    |   GREAT COMPOSERS  |                    |

|                    |   GAMES            |                    |

|                    |   BELLS            |                    |

|                    |   RECORDERS        |                    |

**Figure 20**

**This large pocket chart may be used and re-used for many occasions by merely changing the identifying titles between the pockets.**

# 6

# Music Learning Packets
# for Small Groups
# or Individuals

*Education is that which remains when one has forgotten everything he learned in school.*

Albert Einstein

Music Learning Packets are another effective way to individualize learning activities in the music classroom. The Learning Packet is an objective-based structure that presents the music curriculum in segments (packets) to small groups or individuals. The student is directed through the step-by-step procedure of the packet to learn a specific musical objective by accomplishing activities chosen from the suggested list. It is self-directed and self-paced and is used for reinforcing or further developing a concept which has been presented during large group instruction.

The Music Learning Packet enables the student to complete independently the study of a specific concept through sequentially developed objectives. Bonus or in-depth options supplement each objective to expand musical growth and interest. Each achievement-based objective is a segment of a total musical goal which, combined with other segments, completes a unit of musical study.

Each Music Learning Packet includes a behavioral objective, a list of necessary equipment and materials, a required activity (prerequisite), a list of suggested alternate activities, and an evaluation followed by optional bonus opportunities. These Learning Packets are all teacher-prepared, and each one focuses on a single concept or skill. A time limit is established by the teacher for completion of the packet, based on the student's ability and the complexity of the task involved. Within this limit the student may move at his own pace. The time limit, designed to motivate progress, may be from 15 minutes to several weeks depending upon the musical objective of the packet.

## PRESENTING THE MUSIC LEARNING PACKET

Students who have been teacher-directed for several years will need to learn to make decisions and assume the responsibility for their own learning by first being guided through simple assignments in small groups. By using strategies for Small Group Activities from Performance Day (Chapter 3), Rotation Day (Chapter 4), or Project Day (Chapter 5), you can guide your students toward "readiness" for a Learning Packet.

As an introduction to the use of Learning Packets, it is recommended that the teacher present one packet to the entire class. For this first experience, use a packet that lists several diversified activities. A simple method of presenting the packet quickly is to use the overhead projector to show the students exactly the procedure they may use to complete the packet. Taking time for going through the objective and its alternatives very carefully is well advised. A student needs to know where he is in relation to his objective and where he is expected to go as he completes the objectives. Preparation and readiness are an integral part of the success of the Music Learning Packet system.

The teacher-introduction of the packet may be given to either large or small groups as future occasions demand before you attempt to individualize the assignment. Capitalizing on peer group interaction at this time creates a sounding board for new ideas, reinforces old ideas, encourages the decision-making process, and creates solutions for potential problems. Accountability and sharing are vital in the implementation of the packets and should occur at the completion as well as the beginning of each packet. Group stimulation followed by individualized concentration is a highly motivating style for learning.

For the teacher, virtually all unproductive instruction is eliminated since the alternate activities are designed to meet the interests and needs of the students. A student will find that his ability is stretched, his motivation level high, because he has been required to exact a greater degree of accountability.

Music Learning Packets can be used in any type of group structure.

- Large group instruction may be in progress while one or more students are working on the same or different packets.
- Large groups may be divided, with some students working in a large group while the others are working in small groups or working individually with the same or different packets.
- A small group can be assembled to complete a specific packet for enrichment or remedial work.
- A small group can become one of several teams which rotate from packet to packet.
- Individuals may use a packet during the music class, or they may work outside of the music class and in different parts of the school.
- Several individuals may work independently in the music room while completing the same packet.
- A student may use a packet independently to pursue an area of interest.

Ms. Yates found that using a group as a team worked very well. One day each week she used the Music Learning Packets to reinforce a concept she had previously presented during large group instruction. She divided her students into Tightly Structured Groups and gave each group the same Learning Packet. Each group contained (1) a good reader, (2) a good singer, (3) an instrumental musician, (4) a quiet-passive learner, and (5) an extrovert. With this type of grouping she found that of all the learning bases were covered to build a solid foundation for packet exploration. Each group was encouraged to select different activities. Ms. Yates called this system her Circle of Knowledge because within each group everyone contributed to the activity. At a given time, the entire class re-assembled and each recorder reported to the large group with an account of his group's efforts. Students were encouraged to question and discuss the work of each group; motivation was maintained at a high level. After going through several packets with the small group approach, Ms. Yates found that most of her students were able to work individually with a great degree of success.

## EVALUATING STUDENT PROGRESS

Assessment can be built into the Music Learning Packet in several ways:

- a written evaluation
- a performance
- an oral report
- a student's ability to proceed to the next packet or optional activity
- a product of the packet such as a play, a skit, or a painting.
- a completed worksheet
- a student-taped response
- a conference in small groups
- an individual conference

A sign-up sheet for conferences may be used when the students have completed a packet. One excellent way to assess student progress is a conference using small groups. We recommend that each student sign up for a conference upon completion of each packet. When ten students have finished, a small group conference may be called. During this time materials will be evaluated and student progress will be noted. Using a discussion of the concept involved, you can easily determine which students are ready to move ahead and which students need to be recycled into alternate activities covering the same concept. These conferences can also serve as a test for the effectiveness of the materials and activities used in the packet. Students enjoy sharing their ideas for improvement of the activities during these small group conferences.

To visually chart the progress of a student, a list of required packets may be posted for each month along with a choice of optional ones. As a student progresses from one packet to the next along the continuum of objectives, the entire unit will be completed. Since each Music Learning Packet objective is measurable and since an evaluative feature is contained within each packet, the progress can be easily charted. Student progress may be charted individually, by group, or by a goals task card.

It is recommended that the teacher keep a written record for each student which indicates the amount of student time spent on the packet, the quality of the work, and the use of bonus materials.

## HOW TO WRITE A MUSIC LEARNING PACKET

To dream of suddenly preparing a complete series of Music Learning Packets for every musical objective at every level of learning would be ludicrous. You must begin slowly and use the packets you are able to complete as a supplement to your regular music curriculum. Once you have begun to write your own packets, the job will become easier than it may now seem. You can easily begin today! All you need to do is to develop one packet during this month and one each month for the remainder of the school year. Next year you can refine these packets and begin to create additional ones from a series of sequentially developed objectives using basic concepts in rhythm, melody, and form from your intermediate grade curriculum. We recommend that packets be written without grade level identification so that they can be used at any level.

*Step 1. What is the objective?* The learning objective is very important, and you must be able to isolate it clearly. The easiest place to find learning objectives is in the scope and sequence (often presented in chart form) of any good music curriculum. You may begin by isolating one month's work and proceed to set objectives covering that time span.

The objective should be written in behavioral language, using a low vocabulary level. The objective should answer these questions:

- What concept is the student responsible for developing?
- What musical behavior will the student exhibit?
- What degree of proficiency is expected?
- How will the student demonstrate the proficiency?

Here is an example of a behavorial objective which accomplishes these points: The student will be able to perform at least one new folk dance. The dance will be performed at a level of proficiency that is acceptable to the teacher.

*Step 2. What musical activities or experiences are required to reach the objective?* Each objective should be followed by a list of any pre-requisite activities which are necessary before proceeding to the alternate activities. There may be occasions where pre-requisite activities will be followed by required activities, with other activities optional. The teacher will need to decide which system to use for each particular objective.

*Step 3. What alternate activities will be given for mastering the objective?* Each Music Learning Packet offers alternate activities which are directed toward helping the student learn the objective at his own level of understanding.

- *Learning Levels*

  Each student should have the opportunity to explore a variety of levels, constantly challenging his abilities. Four levels of learning are: (1) Knowledge: naming, recognizing, recalling, listing; (2) Analysis: discovering, differentiating, or examining; (3) Synthesis: creating, performing, composing; (4) Evaluating: judging, concluding, or accepting.

- *Learning Styles*

  There is no "one" style for any student. Use a combination of observation, lecture, talking, experiments, reports, as well as various auditory and visual stimuli.

- *Reading Abilities*

  Use levels of (1) no read, (2) low read, (3) medium read, and (4) high read. Music teachers need to be very careful not to confuse lack of reading skill with lack of musical ability

- *Instructional Modes*

  Some students need explicit directions; some need constant reinforcing of directions. Some students need frequent help, and others work better when left alone.

Each of the alternatives should focus toward the Learning Packet objective.

*Step 4. What materials and equipment are necessary to accomplish the suggested activities?* Each packet should contain a list of all materials and equipment that are required for student use. The teacher must check carefully to be sure that all listed materials are easily accessible before the packets are presented. Packaging all manipulative materials together for each packet will save time.

*Step 5. What type of student assessment/evaluation will be used?* Each Music Learning Packet should include a mastery test or other evaluative event in which the student may demonstrate his degree of proficiency upon completion of the Learning Packet. These evaluative events can be created in a variety of ways. If the student does not meet the expected level, he should be recycled into other activities that will accomplish the same objective. He may be referred to a small group activity, another Learning Packet, or remedial work.

*Step 6. What type of optional or in-depth musical experiences will further motivate and challenge the learner?* Music Learning Packets may include an optional activity which challenges the student to go beyond his present musical knowledge and search for new musical growth. Such options may also be used for remedial work or maintenance of skills. Options might suggest reading a specific book; viewing an audio-tape, film strip, or film; tutoring another student; solving open-ended problems; or investigating physical objects. Options offer opportunities to apply knowledge gained, to develop competencies in areas of interest, or to create a self-designed activity.

## Assembling the Packet

A Music Learning Packet can be a single paper or a series of worksheets placed in an envelope or "packet." All papers necessary for one Learning Packet and its related activities are kept in the packet. Within the packet, pages may be color-coded if the study is extensive, with the activities, assessments, and options each using a different color.

After assembling the packet, consider a system for keeping the materials handy for student use.

- Personal folders can be labeled for each student and filed according to grade and class.
- A group folder can be labeled and used as a small group moves along as a team.

## FIFTEEN SAMPLE MUSIC LEARNING PACKETS

Five Learning Packets using the concept of melody are given here to show you how the sequential progression of objectives can be used to reinforce the isolated concept. Each packet covers one objective, (1) beginning from half steps and (2) progressing to whole steps. Then comes a harder step of (3) distinguishing between half and whole steps, then the (4) development of the major scale, and then (5) chords. Ten packets are single topics to demonstrate how you can reinforce one unit through the Learning Packet system. To help you start writing your own packets, we have given you 30 more ideas. The sample form (Figure 21) will help clarify the necessary steps toward the development of *Your* packet.

### Half Steps in Music

Objective:    The student will be able to visually and aurally recognize half steps with 80 percent accuracy.

Time Limit:    20 minutes

List of Equipment:
Paper/Pencils                     Resonator bells
Music manuscript paper            Recorders
Piano                             Tape recorder
Guitar
Prepared cassette: "Ten Musical Examples of Half Steps / Non-Half Steps"

Pre-Requisite Activity:    Participation in any large group activity or game in which the student is required to identify whole steps and half steps both aurally and visually.

Alternate Activities:    Choose one activity from Group A. Choose one activity from Group B.

A-1.    Make a drawing of a keyboard. Draw arrows to indicate *five* places where half steps occur on the keyboard.

A-2.    Make a drawing of a guitar neck. Draw arrows to indicate *five* places where half steps occur on the neck.

SAMPLE FORM
MUSIC LEARNING PACKET

NAME OF PACKET

OBJECTIVE:

TIME LIMIT:

LIST OF EQUIPMENT:

PRE-REQUISITE ACTIVITY:

ALTERNATE ACTIVITIES:
1.
2.
3.
4.

EVALUATION:

BONUS OPPORTUNITY: (optional)

(directions for proceeding)

**Figure 21**

A-3.   Take a piece of music manuscript paper. Make a treble or bass clef and write pairs of notes that give *five* illustrations of half steps.

B-1   Get paper, pencil, and the cassette "Ten Musical Examples of Half Steps and Non-Half Steps." On your paper, list the numbers one through ten in a column. As you listen to the tape recording, write "Yes" beside the number of each example that is a half step. Write "No" beside the number of each example that is not a half step. Be prepared to give your answer sheet to the teacher.

B-2.   Use the piano to create a game which requires the players to recognize half step sounds. Play the game. Be prepared to demonstrate it for the teacher.

B-3.   Use the guitar to create a game which requires the players to recognize half step sounds. Play the game. Be prepared to demonstrate it for the teacher.

Evaluation:   You will be graded by the quality of your paper work in all of the above activities except B-2 and B-3. In B-2 and B-3 you will be graded on your demonstration.

Bonus Opportunities:   (optional)

***Construct a worksheet which may be used as a test for determining if a student has mastered the concept of seeing and hearing half step sounds.

*** Arrange resonator bells to create a series of twelve continuous half steps. Demonstrate the series for your teacher.

*** Make a tape recording that presents five different examples of half steps in music. Each example should be a set of two tones that are a half step apart. Each example should be performed on a different instrument. You might follow this pattern:

Example 1:   Piano
Example 2:   Guitar
Example 3:   Resonator bells
Example 4:   Recorder
Example 5:   Voice or band instrument

Proceed to the packet on "Whole Steps."

## *Whole Steps in Music*

Objective: The student will be able to visually and aurally recognize whole steps with 80 percent accuracy.

Time Limit: 20 minutes

List of Equipment:
Paper/pencils       Piano
Music manuscript paper       Tape recorder
Recorder       Resonator bells
Guitar or ukulele
Prepared cassette: "Ten Musical Examples of Whole Steps and Non-Whole Steps."

Pre-Requisite Activity: (1) Participation in any large group activity or game which requires the student to recognize whole steps by sight and sound. (2) Completion of Learning Packet: "Half Steps in Music."

Alternate Activities: Choose one activity from Group A and one Activity from Group B.

A-1.      Use the Music Flannelboard to create a game which requires the players to recognize musical steps. Be prepared to demonstrate the game.

A-2.      Compose and notate a 13-note musical compostion which contains only whole-step sounds. Be prepared to show the composition to your teacher.

A-3.      Look at any musical score. With a pencil, lightly draw a circle around every pair of notes which illustrate whole steps in music. Be prepared to show your teacher.

B-1.      Use the piano to demonstrate whole-step sounds in music. Play a series of 11 tones that use only whole-step sounds. Be prepared to play the demonstration for your teacher.

B-2.      Get paper, pencil, and the cassette "Ten Musical Examples of Whole Steps and Non-Whole Steps." On your paper, list the numbers one through ten in a column. As you listen to the tape recording, write "yes" beside the number of each example that is a whole step. Write "no" beside the number of each example that is not a whole step. Be prepared to give your answer sheet to your teacher.

B-3.    Use the guitar or ukulele to create a game which requires the players to recognize whole step sounds. Play the game. Be prepared to demonstrate it for the teacher.

Evaluation:   You will be graded by the quality of your paper work if you chose A-2, A-3, or B-2. If you chose any of the others, your grade will be determined by the quality of your demonstration.

Bonus Opportunities:   (optional)

***Create and demonstrate a game in which the players are required to identify whole steps by sight and sound.

***Use resonator bells to arrange and demonstrate five whole-step patterns.

Proceed to the packet on "Distinguishing Half Steps and Whole Steps."

## Distinguishing Half Steps and Whole Steps

Objective:   The student will be able to aurally and visually distinguish whole steps and half steps with 80 percent accuracy.

Time Limit:   20 minutes

List of Equipment:    Manuscript paper/pencil
Resonator bells
Guitar
Piano
Art supplies as required

Pre-Requisite Activity: (1) Completion of Learning Packets: "Whole Steps in Music" and "Half Steps in Music." (2) Any large group experience requiring the student to distinguish between half steps and whole steps.

Alternate Activities:   Choose one activity from Group A and one activity from Group B.

A-1.    Take a piece of manuscript paper. Write three pairs of notes that illustrate "half steps." Write three pairs of notes that illustrate "whole steps." Label each set appropriately.

A-2. Make a drawing of a keyboard. Draw arrows to indicate three places where half steps occur and three places where whole steps occur. Label each appropriately.

A-3. Make a drawing of a guitar neck. Draw arrows to indicate three places where half steps occur and three places where whole steps occur. Label each appropriately.

B-1. Use some resonator bells to create a game in which players are required to hear half steps and whole steps and identify which ones they hear. Be prepared to demonstrate the game.

B-2. On music manuscript paper, write ten pairs of notes that illustrate half steps and whole steps (include some of each). Be prepared to play the ten examples on the piano and to identify each one as it is played.

B-3. At the guitar, demonstrate three half-step sounds and three whole-step sounds.

Evaluation: Activities from the "A" group will be graded according to the quality of your paper work. Activities from the "B" group will be graded according to the quality of your demonstration.

Bonus Opportunities: (Optional)

*** Prepare a five-minute demonstration/discussion of "Half Steps and Whole Steps on the Piano." Give your demonstration/discussion to a fourth grade music class.

*** Make a poster which illustrates half steps and whole steps. The poster may use guitar, keyboard, or something "far-out!"

Proceed to the packet on "Major Scales."

## Major Scales

Objective: The student will be able to aurally recognize the structural pattern of the major scale; and he will be able to perform at least one major scale.

Time Limit: 10-30 minutes

List of Equipment:

| | |
|---|---|
| Piano | Tape recorder |
| Recorder | Paper/pencil |
| Resonator bells | Multiple copies of any |
| Recording of "Do, Re, Mi" | notated major scale |
| from *Sound of Music* | |

Prepared Cassette: "Ten Musical Examples of Scales/Non-Scales"

Pre-Requisite Activity:   (1) Completion of Learning Packets: "Half Steps," "Whole Steps," "Distinguishing Half Steps and Whole Steps." (2) Participation in any large group experience which has presented the student with the structural pattern of the major scale: "Eight consecutive tones in this arrangement: whole step, whole step, half step, whole step, whole step, whole step, half step."

Alternate Activities:   Choose any two activities.

1.  At the piano, begin on note C and play the major scale.
2.  At the piano, begin on note G and play the major scale.
3.  At the piano, begin on note F and play the major scale.
4.  At the diatonic bells, play the C major scale.
5.  At the resonator bells, play the D major scale.
6.  On a recorder, play the G major scale.
7.  On any band/orchestra instrument, play the major scale of your choice.
8.  Listen to the prepared cassette, "Ten Musical Examples of Scales/Non-Scales." On your paper, list numbers one through ten in a column. As you hear each recorded example, mark your paper "Yes" or "No" according to whether each example is a scale or not. Be prepared to give your answer sheet to the teacher.
9.  Take a copy of a notated major scale and watch it while you listen to a recording of "Do, Re, Mi" from *The Sound of Music*. Circle each scale tone when you hear it. Be prepared to give the paper to the teacher.

Evaluation:   Activities 1-7 will be graded according to your performance. Activities 8-9 will be graded according to the quality of the paper work.

Bonus Opportunities:

*** Find a very easy scale song in a music primer. Learn to play and sing the song. Teach it to a primary class. Tell them it is a major scale.

*** Play one of these major scales on the piano: E, F#, B, or A. Figure it out by yourself.

*** Make a tape recording of yourself playing three different major scales on instruments of your choice.

Proceed to packet on "Chords."

## Chords

Objective:    The student will be able to play, at the piano or bells, the major chords of C, F, and G with 80 percent accuracy.

Time Limit:   15 minutes

List of Equipment:
| | |
|---|---|
| Piano | Tape recorder |
| Diatonic bells | Resonator bells |
| Paper keyboards/pencil | Grease pencil |

Transparent sheets prepared with keyboard pictures

Pre-Requisite Activity:    (1) Completion of Learning Packet, "Major Scales"; (2) Large group demonstration of C Major, F Major, and G Major triads at the piano.

Alternate Activities:    Choose one of these activities.

1. Use a paper keyboard and write "C Chord" on the three appropriate keys, write "F Chord" on the three appropriate keys, and write "G Chord" on the three approptiate keys. Be prepared to give the paper to your teacher.
2. Use a transparent sheet that has been prepared with a keyboard picture. On the sheet write "C Chord," "F Chord," and "G Chord" on all the appropriate keys. Be prepared for the teacher to display your paper on the overhead projector.
3. Make a tape recording of yourself playing chords on the piano. Speak the name of each chord before you play it: "C Chord," "F Chord," "G Chord."

4.  Play chords on the resonator bells. Use three mallets and play C Chord, F Chord, and G Chord. Be prepared to demonstrate them for your teacher.
5.  Play chords on the diatonic bells. Use three mallets and play C Chord, F Chord, and G Chord. Be prepared to demonstrate for the teacher.

Evaluation:   Activities 1-2 will be graded according to the quality of your paper work. Activity 3 will be graded according to your tape recording. Activities 4-5 will be graded according to your demonstration.

Bonus Opportunities:

\*\*\* Play this Chord Composition at the piano:

### CCGGFFGGCCC

\*\*\* Using resonator bells and two other people, do this: Stand around a table. Place one bell from "C Chord" in front of each player. Place one bell from "F Chord" in front of each player. Place one bell from "G Chord" in front of each player. Play the chords together in this pattern: CCC / FFF / GGG / CCC

\*\*\* Create and play a composition which uses only these chords: C Major, F Major, and G Major.


This is the end of this series of five Music Learning Packets. Write your name on the sign-in-sheet to show you have completed this series.


### Orchestral Instruments

Objective:   The student will be able to aurally and visually recognize orchestral instruments with 80 percent accuracy.

Time Limit:   30 minutes

List of Equipment:      Pictures of orchestral instruments
Paper/pencil
Art supplies for constructing mobile
Tape recorder
Resource books; history of instruments

Pre-Requisite Activity: Participation in any experience which dealt with identifying instruments of the orchestra by sight or sound.

Alternate Activities: Choose one activity from the following list.
1. Check your own ability to name all of the pictures of orchestral instruments. Then list as many as you can without looking. Be prepared to give the list to your teacher.
2. Create a game in which players are required to name instruments of the orchestra. Be prepared to demonstrate your game.
3. Make a mobile, to be hung in the music room, which consists of pictures of at least five orchestral instruments.
4. Read about the history of any orchestral instrument of your choice. Be prepared to tell the class at least three historical facts about it.

Evaluation: Each activity will be graded differently:
1. According to your list
2. According to your demonstration
3. According to your finished mobile
4. According to what you tell the class

Bonus Opportunities:
*** Make a tape recording of the sounds of five different orchestral instruments. You may take your examples from any available recordings. Speak the name of each instrument before it is heard. For example, "This is an example of a flute."
*** Play any orchestral instrument for the class. You may play a solo or in a duet or trio.
*** Demonstrate your orchestral instrument for a lower grade. In a five-minute presentation, show how the instrument "works" and play a tune.

(Sign the conference sheet when you have finished this packet.)

*Tape Recorder Music*

Objective: The student will be able to relate two new facts concerning the use of tape recorders in creating musical sounds.

Time Limit: One or two class periods

List of Equipment:    Two reel-to-reel tape recorders
Cassette tape recorders
Tape splicer/splicing tape
Recording of selections of tape recorder music
Sound-filmstrip about the creation of tape recorder music.

Pre-Requisite Activity:   Large group experience in which two reel-to-reel recorders have been used in a demonstration of (1) altering speed of tape, (2) reversing tape, (3) taping sound-on-sound, and (4) altering dynamics. The demonstration should also include splicing, construction of tape loops, and recorded examples of tape recorder music.

Alternate Activities:   Choose one or two partners.
                    Choose one activity.

1. Use a cassette recorder and "collect" any environmental sounds. Make a two-minute tape which uses continuous and changing sounds of all types.
2. Use a cassette recorder and make a tape which is a "Sound Rondo." Decide on a single sound that will be the recurring "A" theme. Put an assortment of different sounds in between. Be sure that each sound begins when the other ends. Your total design will be: ABACADAEAFA
3. Make a tape loop. Use several sounds and about four feet of tape.
4. Use the reel-to-reel recorder. Make a recording and alter the speed.
5. Use two reel-to-reel recorders. Make a recording in which you alter the speed four times.
6. Use the reel-to-reel recorder. Make a recording and then play the sounds in reverse.
7. Use a cassette recorder and record sounds which illustrate a simple story or situation. Use no words. Make the tape about 60 seconds long.
8. View the Sound filmstrip which is available. Make a list of three facts learned from the film.
9. Listen to recordings of two selections of tape recorder music. On a paper write (1) the names of the compositions, (2) names of their composers, and (3) a sentence about the composition.

Evaluation: Activities 1-7 will be graded according to the finished tape. Activities 8-9 will be graded according to your paper.

Bonus Opportunities: (optional)
*** Bring a recording from home of a composition for tape recorder. Play it for the class and tell something about it.
*** With your teacher's permission you may do any activity listed above which you have not done before.
*** Create a composition of taped music sounds using a combination of several techniques used in Activities 3, 4, and 5. Play it for your class.
*** Look in your music textbook to determine if there is any information given concerning music for tape recorders. If there is, do investigate it!

(Sign the conference sheet when you have finished this packet.)

*Till Eulenspiegel*

Objective: The student will be able to recognize the main theme and the main story-line from the program music "Till Eulenspiegel" and be able to contribute to a class discussion.

Time Limit: One or two class periods

List of Equipment: Tape recorder
Recording, "Till Eulenspiegel"
Play script, "Till Eulenspiegel"
Reference books about Richard Strauss
Prepared worksheet about Richard Strauss
Art supplies as required for picture/poster making
Sound-filmstrip about "Till Eulenspiegel"

Pre-Requisite Activity: Large group presentation of the story and music, "Till Eulenspiegel's Merry Pranks," composed by Richard Strauss.

Alternate Activities: Choose one activity from the following list.
1. Work with some other students to illustrate all of the incidents in the story. Plan and make pictures for all of the music. Some

pictures may be repeated. Be prepared to share your pictures and to correlate them with the music.

2. Prepare the play "Till Eulenspiegel" with some other students. Present the play to the class.

3. Read about Richard Strauss in reference books provided. Complete the worksheet about him. Give the worksheet to the teacher.

4. Make a tape recording of the following exerpts from "Till Eulenspiegel": (1) French horn playing main theme, (2) Till's "mischief" theme, (3) Till in love, and (4) Till in the market place. Identify each excerpt on the tape. Prepare your tape to give to the teacher.

Evaluation:   Grades will be earned as follows:
1. According to the pictures and their correlation
2. According to the play and its presentation
3. According to the worksheet and its completeness
4. According to the tape recording and its accuracy

Bonus Opportunities:
*** Prepare a poster (suitable for bulletin board) concerning "Till Eulenspiegel."
*** View the sound-filmstrip about "Till Eulenspiegel."

(Sign the conference sheet when you have completed this packet.)

### Till Eulenspiegel

List of Characters:
  Narrator
  Till Eulenspiegel
  Father
  Sellers (any number)
  Market woman
  Burgomaster
  Villagers (any number)
  Milk girl
  Professors (any number)
  Judge
  Watchman

Narrator:   This is a story of the merry adventures of Till Eulenspiegel. Till was a mischievous fellow. Never was there a lad who so delighted in playing jokes and pranks as did the fun-loving Till. His fame as a prankster was known far and wide throughout the land.

Till would wander, this way and that, wherever his fancy took him, ever seeking new adventures. Sometimes he would stay in one place several days, sometimes as long as a month. But it was never very long before the roguish lad would be boldly on his way in quest of new fun.

Children loved him. They knew that there was always lots of laughter when Till was near. But, as you may well understand, the grown-ups would become very angry with him. Especially when the joke was on them. (Curtain opens)

Children:   Till, I wish you would stay. It's always fun when you're in town.

Father:   Till, when are you ever going to grow up?

Till:   I never harm anyone. It is just that people have forgotten how to laugh.

Narrator:   One day Till mounted his horse and galloped off on his first adventure. It was market day, and the square was filled with stands and booths.

Sellers:   Bonnets, stockings, clothes of all descriptions!
Bananas, figs, apples, and oranges,
Chickens (cluck, cluck), geese (quack).
Get your supper for tonight!

Till:   (aside) Just look at all those silly people arguing and yelling. I think it's time for some excitement.

Narrator:   Without warning Till cracked his whip and spurred his horse into a fast gallop. Then with a loud cry that frightened all the people, Till plunged into the market place. The horse and his mischievous rider knocked everything down.

Market Woman:   It's Till Eulenspiegel. Come back here, you rascal. See what you've done. Who's going to pay for my lost chickens?

Till:     Ha, Ha, Ha!

Narrator:  Till traveled a short distance to the next town. He then remembered . . .

Till:     I caused so much trouble in the market that the villagers got mad. Oh, no! I remember what the Burgomaster said.

Burgomaster:   If we catch you here again, into jail you go!

Till:     I'm not ready for jail. I know what I'll do. I'll disguise myself. (Thinking) I have it! I'll dress as a priest. No one will ever suspect that a holy man would really be Till Eulenspiegel.

Narrator:  So Till put on a long, black coat, turned his white collar around, and promptly continued into town. As Till passed through the village, the village folk removed their hats respectfully.

Till:     Bless you, my children.

Villagers:   Thank you, Father.

Narrator:  Now Till decided not to remain there too long or he would perchance say something to ruin his disguise. So, after delivering a short sermon, he continued on his way.

Till:     What an awful thing to pretend to be a holy man. Never again will I play a trick like that.

Narrator:  In a short while Till had forgotten the incident and was back to his old tricks.
          One day, while riding along a country road, he saw a maiden carrying milk to market.

Till:     A fine day to you, pretty miss.

Milk girl:   A pleasant day to you, too.

Till:     Your pails of milk are heavy. Let me help you.

Milk girl:   Thank you, good sir, but I can carry them quite well myself.

Narrator:  Till was not used to being refused. He tried again and again, but without success. This only made Till more attracted to the maiden. Finally Till could not stand her cold manner any longer.

Till:     Marry me maiden and I will stop my wanderings and tricks.

Milk girl:   (Laughs and runs off)

Till:     Very well, you will never again have the chance of marrying so excellent a lad as Till Eulenspiegel.

Narrator:   One day, Till met a group of wise men who were journeying to the University to attend a meeting of learned professors.

Till:     (aside) Ah, these men in their black robes and spectacles think they are wiser than everyone else because they always have their heads buried in books. We shall see if, with all their knowledge, they also have sharp wits.

Narrator:   And so the crafty lad made believe that he, too, was a great scholar.

Till:     Good day, learned professors. May a humble student have the pleasure of your company?.

Narrator:   The professors looked at Till but continued their talking. Finally Till entered the conversation pretending to speak the ancient Greek language.

Professors:   Is it possible that this boy knows more than we do? Perhaps he is wiser than we are?

Narrator:   Finally Till got tired of teasing and he rode away laughing.

Narrator:   Till journeyed for months. One day, when the cold November wind was blowing, Till came to a town which was famous for its harsh treatment of pranksters. He remembered the harsh treatment and narrow escape he had during his last visit to this town. He remembered . . .

Judge:   (offstage) If you set foot in this town again, you will be severely punished.

Narrator:   But Till was cold, hungry, and very tired.

Till:     What sort of life is this? I have no home . . . just always wandering around.

Narrator:   Suddenly his face brightened up.

Till:       I know what kind of life. A short and merry one. Has anyone had more fun than I? What sport it has been, playing tricks on fat shopkeepers and dull-witted burgomasters. Living one's life in one place is for simpletons . . . not for the great Till Eulenspiegel.

Narrator:   So Till continued to the town.

Till:       The town watchmen here are a dull-witted lot. Much too stupid to notice me.

Narrator:   Hardly had he passed the town entrance when he heard a voice cry.

Watchman:   TILL EULENSPIEGEL!

Narrator:   Till was so surprised at the town watchman that before he could run    . he was arrested.

Narrator:   Till was brought before the court. The judges took their places looking very, very solemn in the crowded court room.

Judge:      Bring the prisoner here.

Narrator:   Till stood before the judges. Can you see the old mocking, defiant smile on his face?

Till:       (aside) I'll talk myself out of this just like I did the last time.

Judge:      Till Eulenspiegel! You are accused of having disobeyed the orders of this court! You were warned never to return.

Till:       Most honorable judges, I beg you permit me to say a word in my behalf.

Narrator:   The judges would not listen. The chief of the judges banged his gavel once more. Then the judges whispered among themselves for a few minutes.

Judge:      Till Eulenspiegel! It is the judgement of this court that for punishment . . . you be hanged.

Narrator:   Now for the first time Till realized that it was serious.

Till:       Hanged? They want to take my life? I'm just a little boy having fun.

Narrator:   The judges refused to listen.

Judge:   Till Eulenspiegel! It is the sentence of this court that you be hanged.

Till:   But, but . . . my life . . .

Narrator:   Till was carried away. His voice became weaker and weaker. Till was placed on the gallows, and there he died.

### *Johann Sebastian Bach*

Objective:   The student will be able to relate at least two facts about the life and works of Johann Sebastian Bach.

Time Limit:   One or two class periods

List of Equipment:
Recording, "Little Fugue in G Minor" (organ)
Reference book for student use containing discussion of fugue.
Sound-filmstrip concerning life and works of Bach
Prepared worksheet correlated with the sound-filmstrip
Recording, "Joy of Man's Desiring" (organ)
Recording, "Joy of Man's Desiring" (Rock group: Apollo)
Reference books on J. S. Bach for student use
Art supplies as required for poster

Pre-Requisite Activity:   None

Alternate Activities:   Choose one from the following list.
1.   Listen to the recording, "Little Fugue in G Minor." Read the discussion in the book about the fugue. Listen again to the recording; this time use a colored pencil to make a mark on a paper each time that the main theme (subject) is heard. Count the total number of entries; give the paper to your teacher.
2.   View the sound-filmstrip about the life of Bach. Complete the worksheet that accompanies it.
3.   Listen to the organ recording, "Joy of Man's Desiring." Listen to the Apollo recording, "Joy of Man's Desiring." Write a report in which you answer these questions: How does the melody compare? How does the rhythm compare? How does the harmony compare?
4.   Make a poster containing four illustrated facts about Bach's life or music.

5. Use the reference books. Make a list of five important questions (and answers) about Bach's life or music.

Evaluation:     Activities 1, 2, 3, and 5 will be graded according to the quality of your paper work. Activity 4 will be graded according to the quality of your poster.

Bonus Opportunities:   (optional)
   \*\*\* Get together with some others and act out one or more scenes from the life of J. S. Bach.
   \*\*\* Bring a recording from home and play a selection of Bach's music. Be prepared to say something about it.
   \*\*\* Find an example of Bach's music in any music book. Play or sing it for the class (solo, duet, or trio.)

(Sign the conference sheet when you have finished this packet.)

## The Rhythm of Africa

Objective:     The student will be able to name at least three distinctive features of African music.

Time Limit:   Two class periods

List of Equipment:
   Drums of various kinds
   Several different music textbooks
   Art supplies as required for mural
   Magazines, books, articles concerning African music
   Pattern for African Dakishi
   Recordings:
      "Music of Equatorial Africa," *Folkways* P 402
      "Drums of the Yoruba of Nigeria," *Folkways* P 441
      "Songs of the Watusi," *Folkways* P 428

Pre-Requisite Activity:   View a film about the distinctive characteristics of African music.

Alternate Activities:   Choose one activity from the following list.
   1. Draw and identify three of the following African instruments: mbira (thumb piano), musical bow, drum, xylophone, flute.

2. Listen to a recording of African music. List the instruments that you hear.
3. Get a group together to form an African Drum Ensemble. Ask your teacher to help you in getting started.
4. Practice a drumming pattern that you can play along with a recording of African music.
5. Make a mural showing at least three ways that African music has affected American music.
6. Construct a musical instrument that is patterned after an African instrument. (This will need to be done primarily at home.)
7. Practice and perform an African drumming pattern.
8. Read about African music from resource materials; write a brief report on what you read.

Evaluation:

Activities 1, 2, 5, and 8 will be graded on the quality of your work and the accuracy of detail.

Activities 3, 4, and 7 will be graded on your performance or demonstration.

Activity 6 will be graded on the creativeness displayed in your instrument.

Bonus Opportunities:   (optional)

***Construct an African Dakishi

***Search music textbooks to find music from Africa.

***Create your own "African drumming pattern" and notate it.

(Sign the conference sheet when you have finished this packet.)

## The Science of Sound

Objective:   The student will be able to demonstrate knowledge of pitch, loudness, or quality through an experiment in sound.

Time Limit:   Two class periods

List of Equipment:

Sound-filmstrip on "The Science of Sound"

Resource materials on experimentation of sound

Tuning fork

Tuned glasses, drinking straws, soda bottles, test tubes, or other
materials necessary to make instruments.

Materials necessary for experimentation

Pre-Requisite Activity:   Viewing a sound-filmstrip on "The Science
of Sound"

Alternate Activities:   Choose one activity from the following list.
1.  Experiment with a rubber band, paper strips, and a tuning fork
to conclude that sounds are produced by vibrations.
2.  Create an experiment to determine how sound waves travel
through a substance.
3.  Using a table, the air, water, your head, and a cord, determine
which materials transmit sound most effectively.
4.  Read about how sound is focused and absorbed. Use the music
room to see if any materials mentioned in your reading are
found as a source of absorption. Make a list of these materials.
5.  Make a "homemade" instrument to demonstrate the principle
of a vibrating column of air.
6.  Choose an orchestral or band instrument and prepare a demonstration for your class showing the method of sound produc-
tion.
7.  Research and give a report on "How a Recording Is Made."
8.  Make a written report on "How Does a Voice Sing?"

Evaluation:

Activities 1, 2, 3, and 5 will be graded on the quality of the finished
experiment and accuracy of demonstration.

Activity 4 will be graded on thoroughness and accuracy of the
prepared list.

Activity 6 will be graded on the quality of the demonstration.

Activity 7 will be graded on the accuracy and quality of presentation.

Activity 8 will be graded on the quality of the research.

Bonus Opportunities:   (optional)
***Research and give a report on ultrasonic sound and its applica-
tion to music.
***Using a decibel meter, collect sounds around the school to
determine sources of sound pollution.

\*\*\* Research and write a report on sound pollution around your neighborhood.

\*\*\* Make a demonstration model of the human ear and show your class how it receives the sound.

(Sign the conference sheet when you have completed this packet.)

## Folk Instruments

Objective:    The student will be able to name and recognize four folk instruments from different countries.

Time Limit:   Two class periods

List of Equipment:
Music textbooks containing ballads and folk-hero songs
Resource materials on folk instruments
Kazoos
Washboards
Tub bass
Bottles
Materials for environmental instruments (coconuts, walnuts, thimbles, rocks, and so on)

Pre-Requisite Activities:   None

Alternate Activities:   Choose one activity from the following list.
1.  Choose a country and research the type of folk instrument most commonly used.
2.  Choose a folk-hero song and determine an appropriate folk instrument to accompany the song.
3.  Choose a ballad and accompany it with a guitar or autoharp.
4.  Create an instrument (folk-style) for accompanying a simple folk song of your choice. The instrument must be made of materials found in your environment.
5.  Research American folk instruments and see how many different instruments you can list.
6.  Write a report on the evolution of the mandolin from the early day lute.
7.  Create an ensemble to accompany a folk song of your choice using a kazoo, a washboard, a tub bass, and a set of tuned bottles.

Evaluation:
> Activities 1, 2, 5, and 6 will be graded on the quality of your report.
>
> Activities 3 and 7 will be graded on your performance.
>
> Activity 4 will be graded on the creativeness of your instrument and its appropriateness for accompaniment.

Bonus Opportunities: (optional)
> *** Write a play about early America and incorporate folk instruments, showing their role in society.
>
> *** Create a dulcimer from a kit.
>
> *** Research and give a report on the use of folk instruments in popular music today.

(Sign the conference sheet when you have completed this packet.)

## *Structures in Music*

Objective:    The student will be able to aurally identify two structures in music (ternary and rondo) with 80 percent accuracy.

Time Limit:   Two class periods

List of Equipment:
> Art supplies
> Recordings of ternary and rondo form
> Classroom instruments
> Resource books with chants

Pre-Requisite Activities:   Participation in any experience which dealt with identification of structures in music.

Alternate Activities:   Choose one activity from Group A and one activity from Group B.

> A-1.    Create a graphic display to symbolize ternary form by cutting paper shapes and gluing them to a sheet of manila paper.
>
> A-2.    Choose a recording from the selection provided and pantomime a ternary form.
>
> A-3.    Choose a recording from the selection provided and create a dance which demonstrates ternary form.

A-4.   Create a game which can be used in class to demonstrate ternary form.

A-5.   Choose two friends and create a way to demonstrate ternary form without using any movement.

B-1.   Create a graphic display to symbolize rondo form by cutting paper shapes and gluing them to a sheet of manila paper.

B-2.   Using only body sounds, create a rondo form and tape record your composition.

B-3.   Choose a chant from the resource materials and use it for the "A" part of your rondo. Use different classroom instruments for the other sections.

B-4.   Create a game to demonstrate rondo form.

B-5.   Create a dance to demonstrate rondo form.

Evaluation:

Activities A-1 and B-1 will be graded on the accuracy of your display.

Activities A-2, A-3, A-4, A-5, B-2, B-3, B-4, and B-5 will be graded on the quality of your research and the quality of your demonstration.

Bonus Opportunities:   (optional)

*** Bring a recording from home to play for the class and be able to determine if it is ternary or rondo.

*** Listen to the radio and report to the class the name of a pop tune that is in ternary form.

*** Tape a rondo composition using environmental sounds.

(Sign the conference sheet when you have completed this packet.)

## Folk Dances of the World

Objective:   The students will be able to perform, at a level of proficiency acceptable to the teacher, a folk dance from one country and have knowledge of the use of folk dances in other countries.

Time Limit:   Two class periods

List of Equipment:

Recordings of folk dances from around the world

Resource materials for dances in other countries, directions for performing dances, and the history of the dance.

Pre-Requisite Activities:    Participation in any folk dance group experience.

Alternate Activities:   Choose one activity from Group A and one activity from Group B.

A-1.     Form a group of eight and choose either a square dance, a round dance, or a line dance from the resources available. Teach it to yourselves and be able to demonstrate it for the large group.

A-2.     Form a group of eight and use a dance which has the directions given through the song. Teach it to yourselves and be able to demonstrate it for the large group.

A-3.     Form a group of eight and dance a square dance, with one person as the "caller." Follow his directions.

A-4.     Form a group of eight and create your own folk-type dance steps. Choose a folk song from your music book for the dance.

B-1.     Using the resource material provided, choose a country and report on the type of dances characteristic of this country. Give your report to your class.

B-2.     Using the resource material provided, research and draw the costumes of a country of your choice which are worn while doing a folk dance.

B-3.     Write a report on locations in the United States where you would find groups participating in authentic folk dancing.

B-4.     Research and show to the class reproductions of famous paintings which depict folk dancing.

Evaluation:

Activities A-1, A-2, A-3, and A-4 will be graded on the performance.

Activities B-2 and B-3 will be graded on the quality of the research.

Activities B-1 and B-4 will be graded on the quality of the research and the presentation of the report.

Bonus Opportunities:   (optional)

*** Write a report on the events from history which occurred during the time that a specific folk dance was popular.

*** Bring a guest lecturer to class who has experience in folk dancing.

*** View a video-tape or sound-filmstrip on folk dances from other countries.

(Sign the conference sheet when you have completed this packet.)

### The Musical Theater

Objective: The student will be able to differentiate between musical theater and grand opera with 80 percent accuracy and will be able to demonstrate knowledge of how an opera or a musical is created.

Time Limit: Three class periods

List of Equipment:
Art supplies as necessary
Resource materials for musical theater and grand opera
Recordings of slected musicals and operas
Libretto for selected musicals and operas (if appropriate)
A sound-filmstrip on the American musical theater
Stories of the more famous operas and musicals
Reference books on composers

Pre-Requisite Activities: Participation in a large group experience on the musical theater. Working knowledge of grand operas.

Alternate Activities: Choose one activity from the following list.
1. View a film strip on the American musical theater and complete the worksheet provided.
2. Create a miniature set for the musical of your choice. First determine the musical and then the scene you wish to create.
3. Construct several puppets to sing a scene from your favorite musical. Choose a friend to work with.
4. Listen to a musical and tell the story to the class.
5. Choose a musical and report on the composer and the lyricist.
6. Dramatize a scene from your favorite musical. Choose several friends to help you.

Evaluation:
Activity 1 will be graded on the accuracy of the worksheet.

Activity 2 will be graded on the accuracy and skill demonstrated in the construction of the set.

Activity 3 will be graded on the creativeness of your puppets and the appropriateness of the characterizations during performance.

Activities 4 and 5 will be graded on the quality of your report.

Activity 6 will be graded on the quality and accuracy of your dramatization.

Bonus Opportunities:　(optional)

*** Create your own musical. Work with several of your friends and present it to your class.

*** Create a filmstrip series following a story line from a musical of your choice.

*** Write a report on the development of the musical theater in America.

(Sign the conference sheet when you have completed the packet.)

## THIRTY MORE IDEAS FOR MUSIC LEARNING PACKETS

1. Any Music Concept or Competency

   For these packets choose concepts of rhythm, melody, harmony, form, tone color, or expression or choose a competency of singing or playing an instrument.

2. The Development of Jazz

   This packet could be a historical approach, a listening approach, or a performance.

3. Performers of Pop Music

   Students can research performers biographically, make style comparisons, or demonstrate listening skills.

4. Homemade Instruments

   Collections of boxes, cans, and all sorts of "junk" can be used to make instruments. Students can perform solos or in ensemble, or they can use the instruments for acoustical study.

5. American Folk Music

   A packet on folk music can take several directions, including researching, listening, creating, and performing.

6.  Opera

    Operas are fun to create and perform. Some students enjoy the stage and technical aspect while others prefer to attend one.

7.  Experimental Music

    This topic is often overlooked and makes a perfect packet. Students feel free to create and perform compositions in these small groups.

8.  Improvisation (Vocal and Instrumental)

    Students who are musically interested and have skill in an instrument or voice enjoy experimenting with improvisation. This is a good outgrowth of your jazz unit.

9.  Ballet

    Many students who study dance privately choose this packet. There are also students who prefer to listen to the music or attend a performance.

10. Careers in Music

    A packet on careers can go in many directions. Students can research, interview, bring guests to class, or create a new career in music.

11. Composition Using the Diatonic Scales

    This packet is particularly effective following the packets on melody concepts. Students enjoy using their band and orchestra instruments as well as classroom instruments.

12. Creating an Instrumental Ensemble (or Vocal)

    A polished performance is not necessary in the completion of this packet. Students can write one for their band or orchestra instruments and then perform or create one as they play.

13. Experience Stories

    Experience stories are fun to create and perform.

14. Music from Other Countries

    Packets such as this go along beautifully with social studies units. Students can research folk dances, composers' use of folk songs in composition, singing folk songs, or identifying rhythmic or tonal characteristics.

15. Composers

    At any grade level a specific composer or a group of similar composers can be isolated for study (listening, dramatizing, singing, creating similar styles, biographical sketches, or performing).

16. Music of Other Ethnic Groups

    Students enjoy listening and performing as well as creating similar folk songs. Use appropriate instruments for accompaniment or make your own.

17. Great Works of Music Literature

    A carefully guided packet in listening is very effective. Be sure to give many identifying characteristics along the way to encourage careful listeners. Program music is a real winner for this packet.

18. History of Music

    This packet can start from the present and move backward in time or vice-versa. Listening and styles are important so that not all is research history.

19. Program Music

    Most students enjoy program music and learn to identify it quickly. Try guided listening, studying the composer, studying the era, dramatizing, and performing themes.

20. Pop Music

    Pop music is general enough to include "top-forty" performers and orchestral pop music. It can include styles from country and western to rock.

21. Synthesizers

    Many schools have access to small synthesizers or students can take field trips to see one. If not, the principles of synthesized sound make fascinating research, and most music textbooks have a unit of study on this.

22. Environmental Composition

    Taping or reproducing sounds of our environment make good compositions. Students can become quite adept in making tape loops and altering sound.

23. Sound Pollution

    This packet can cover (1) the problem of sound pollution, (2) where it occurs, and (3) proposed solutions. Students can tape different sound pollutants and make compositions, have lectures from environmentalists, or use a decibel meter to find possible pollution.

24. The Development of Musical Notation
   This packet interests students in researching our present notation and then developing a new system.
25. Types of Dances
   Dances such as the waltz, mazurka, polka, Charleston, or jitterbug all reflect countries or eras within one country. These are fun to learn to perform and go along with other units or songs effectively.
26. Theme and Variations
   Theme and Variations can be performed as a creative experience or used as a listening or "great works" packet.
27. Twelve-Tone Row
   A packet on compositional techniques works effectively as students discover the "how-to" of a twelve-tone row. A less creative student may want to listen to compositions or research a composer.
28. Polytonality
   Performance is a challenging packet objective. By using simple melodies, a student can create and tape a performance. Other ideas can be listening or composers or perhaps combining with polyrhythms.
29. The Use of Folk Music in Classical Music Literature
   As a culminating-type packet, from either folk music or program music, students can listen and isolate familiar melodies. Skillful listeners can learn to identify specific countries by the characteristics of the melody.
30. Music for Television and Movies
   This can be one or several packets. Students can listen, identify, research, analyze, or create.

# 7

*One-Hundred and Thirty*
*Music Contracts*
*for Individual Activities*

*No one knows what it is that he can do*
*until he tries.*

Publican Syrus

A Music Contract is a learning plan designed by the individual student in which he selects and declares what he will undertake, when it will be completed, and the way in which it will be assessed. When the teacher and the student agree on the contract, the student begins working at his own pace, choosing his materials and the method of learning. When he has finished the contract, the student records the date of completion and suggests a grade for his contract. The student then submits his finished work or indicates that his performance/demonstration is ready to be shared.

A contract may be used for in-depth study of a specific music topic, for enrichment of a previously learned topic, or for gaining new knowledge. A contract may include both concepts and performance competencies. The learning content is selected by the student from teacher-made options, or it may be designed by the student. As a student selects his topic and the materials for his chosen goal, he has personalized the entire learning process. This type of music contract is not pre-programmed to channel the student in a sequential lock-step pattern, but is designed to give the student the freedom to learn about music in a way that is meaningful to him. You should find that when you have carefully prepared your students for this freedom of individual learning by the step-by-step procedure of the preceeding months, they will be "ready" and business-like with their learning process. Your role is to make sure that each contract presents a unique and intriguing challenge for the student.

In the actual case stories of Tony, David, Susan, and Dawn which follow, it can be seen how the opportunity to select or design a personal contract can be quite meaningful in a student's work. Sometimes the meaningfulness of the experience may go beyond the walls of the music room. When that happens, music education is enjoying its finest moments.

Tony was a student who sat through every music class with a distant look about him. He spoke only when spoken to, and even then he was not always "in tune" with the conversation or discussion. When his teacher presented the opportunity for him to write his own contract, he became instantly interested. He considered all of the assignments offered and finally decided to compose a sixteen-note melody for bells. He was happy to work alone; he never had done well working with others. Tony enjoyed creating music with the bells because he never had time to do that during regular music class; and he was delighted to use the new sound booth which was available for tape recording. When he had finished, he was anxious to take the completed tape recording home for his Dad to hear . . . especially with the good comments the teacher had written. Tony's father was so proud of him.

David has come to a new land recently from India. He was a conscientious student, but as yet had no friends. His family life was so different from everyone else's that he was simply estranged from the classroom socially. An opportunity to design his own contract on the music of India changed that. David brought pictures and recordings from home. He explained the meanings of the songs; he described the instruments; and, greatest of all, he won the respect of his classmates. The teacher called it a musical miracle.

Susan was having a love affair with her bass violin. Learning to play that instrument seemed more important to her than anything else in the world just now! The bass was always there at school, but Susan was permitted to play it only during orchestra class and sometimes after school. When her music teacher assigned the students to write their own music contracts, Susan knew that her contract would include her string bass. She waited patiently as the teacher outlined many possible assignments. Not a single assignment mentioned using a bass! But Susan was heartened when, at the end, the teacher finally said, ". . . or create your own assignment." Susan did. She wrote a note on every line and space of the bass clef. Then she named and played each note. She had planned to tape record it; but when she was practicing everybody gradually stopped their work to watch her. At the end they all applauded and the teacher said that a tape recording wouldn't be necessary after such a magnificent performance. Susan planned, right there, to write a letter to her Grandma telling about this happy experience, but not before she chose another music contract using her bass violin.

Sharing something special with her classmates was just the motivation Dawn needed. Using recordings from her father's collection meant a lot to her. Dawn's father was a music professor at the University, and she felt so privileged when he allowed her to share his collection. After Dawn had completed one music contract about "Music as a Cultural Expression," she decided to design an assignment that utilized her father's recordings. She simply assigned herself to tape record the main theme from five nineteenth-century operatic overtures. She had seen several operas; the work would be fun; and she wouldn't mind the extra homework at all. This opportunity just filled a need in her life at that time. She thought that she could finish easily in one week. And Dawn felt certain that she would be proud to share her work with her classmates. Sharing with classmates was what made it a neat idea!

## Keeping the System

It is desirable for each student to have his own personal file folder in which to keep a music contract record sheet and all completed written assignments. (The student may be requested to supply a file folder along with other school supplies.) Each folder should be clearly labeled; and each student should be responsible for maintaining an accurate, up-to-date record of his completed contracts as well as any resulting papers.

When the music contract record sheet and written assignments are kept in each student's personal folder, evaluation by the teacher is facilitated. Examination of the contents of the folder and its music contract record sheet completes the teacher's assessment of student progress in the contract program, except for evaluations of performances/demonstrations, which can easily be done at the time they are shared.

A file drawer or a box labeled for each class can house the personal music folders. The sign-up sheet for performance/demonstration may be placed near the file.

| | MUSIC CONTRACT RECORD SHEET | | | | | |
|---|---|---|---|---|---|---|
| | Name _____ | | | | | |
| | Homeroom _____ | | | | | |
| Contract Number or Description | Will the result of this Contract be a *Paper* or a *Performance?* (or other?) | Beginning Date | Completion Date | Grade | Teacher's Comments | |
| | | | | | | |

**Figure 22**

## STUDENT INFORMATION

### Procedure for Music Contract Work Day

1. Select any two contracts from those offered; only one of your choices may require a musical instrument.
2. List your two choices on your music contract record sheet.
3. Complete the music contract record sheet as much as possible (write "paper" or "performance" and beginning date).
4. Begin working on one of your contract choices.
5. When you have completed your contract do the following:
    a) If you have completed a paper, place it in your personal music folder.
    b) If you have prepared a performance or demonstration, write your name on the paper designated.
    c) Write the completion date and your suggested grade on your music contract record sheet.
6. Begin at once to work on your other contract selection.
7. After completing both contracts, begin again with item one (above).

REMEMBER:

*Your daily grade is based on your personal work habits. Keep busy!

**The object of this program is to complete as many contracts as possible. Unlimited opportunity!

To help you facilitate the idea of each student working on an individual project, several things may be kept in mind.

- A limited number of available musical instruments will help to control the sound level of the classroom. A selection of about four each of recorders, diatonic bells, and ukuleles has worked successfully.
- Assignments involving the use of a tape recorder should probably not be undertaken unless there is a sound-proof area that can be used while the recording is being made.
- Multiple copies of musical scores should be readily available for student use. Duplication of folk songs from old music books satisfies this need nicely.
- Appointing two or three advanced students as "Teacher Assis-

tants'' to aid other students with scales, chords, and so on has proven to be a helpful idea.

- Be sure to provide plenty of music manuscript paper. A half-sheet will be enough for most student assignments, so you will probably wish to provide half-sheets.

## ONE-HUNDRED THIRTY SUGGESTED CONTRACT ASSIGNMENTS

The ideas for contract assignments are organized into four units: Linear Sound, Vertical Sounds, Techniques Used in Music Compositions, and Music as a Cultural Expression. We have presented these four units so that you can present each one during a different term of the school year if you wish. As you gain experience in working with contracts in your music classes, you will discover *your* best way for implementing the program. Allow some time for experimenting and discovering. Chances are good that you will find many ways to adapt, expand, and improve these assignments. When that happens, this book will have accomplished one of its prime objectives.

### Subject: Linear Sound

Linear Sound may be defined as any aurally or visually perceived horizontal line in music. Single-note melodies and chants are studied, created, and performed, and scales and intervals are studied. No study of chords or chord-producing instruments appears here because this unit deals only with linear sound—single tones advancing along a horizontal line. Invite your students to design additional projects dealing with linear sound. They may suggest more ideas for voices, orchestral instruments, or ways for discovering certain types of melodies that exist in music literature.

Directions: Consider the following assignments. Select one or design one of your own.

1. Using bells, play a new song "by ear."
2. Using bells, play a new song by reading the music.
3. On a music staff, write a note and its name on each line and space.
4. Prepare a demonstration in which you name and play the following musical examples on a piano:

five notes that illustrate "stepping up"
five notes that illustrate "stepping down"
five notes that illustrate "skipping up"
five notes that illustrate "skipping down"

5.  Using a page of a musical score, demonstrate your knowledge of left to right progression by drawing a single pencil line which connects the notes in the proper order.
6.  On line one of a sheet of music manuscript paper, write an original row of 16 notes. On line two write another row of notes identical to the first. On line three write a row of 16 notes which is not identical to the first two rows.
7.  Using music manuscript paper, write the major scales of C, F, and G.
8.  Using music manuscript paper, write the minor scales of D, A, and E.
9.  Write any three major scales other than C, F, and G.
10.  Write any three minor scales other than D, A, and E.
11.  Write the A major scale and its parallel minor.
12.  Write the D major scale and its parallel minor.
13.  Write any major scale and its parallel minor except A or D.
14.  Play any major scale on any pitched instrument.
15.  Play any minor scale on any pitched instrument.
16.  Write eight examples of intervals of the 2nd.
17.  Write eight examples of intervals of the 3rd.
18.  Write eight examples of intervals of the 4th.
19.  Play on any pitched instrument any intervals of the 2nd.
20.  Play on any pitched instrument any intervals of the 3rd.
21.  Play on any pitched instrument any intervals of the 4th.
22.  Using any musical score, circle all examples of intervals of the 2nd.
23.  Using any musical score, circle all examples of intervals of the 3rd.
24.  Using any musical score, circle all examples of intervals of the 4th.
25.  Using any three bells, create a ten-note melody and notate it in whole notes.
26  Using the scores of any four American folk songs, circle any of the following note-patterns that you find. Identify the

circled notes by writing the number (or syllable) of the scale
tone beneath each note.

Patterns to find:

| | | | |
|---|---|---|---|
| 5 2 | 1 3 5 | 1 8 | 3 2 1 |
| 5 3 1 | 8 6 5 | 1 2 3 | 5 4 3 |
| 3 5 1 | 5 6 5 | 5 3 | 1 2 1 |
| 3 4 5 | 3 5 | 8 7 8 | 8 7 6 5 |
| 1 5 | 4 3 2 1 | | |

27. Create a simple dance in which you illustrate the rise and fall
of the melody in the accompanying music.

28. Sing any song as a solo for the class, taking time to enunciate
distinctly and to breathe properly.

29. Using a music staff, write all of the notes of the treble staff;
name them and play them on piano or bells.

30. Using the bells of a pentatonic scale, create a ten-note melody
and perform it.

31. Using the bells of a pentatonic scale, create a ten-note melody
and notate it.

32. Play any melody "by ear" on the recorder.

33. Play any melody "by note" on the recorder.

34. Using the bells for any major scale, create a 16-note melody
and play it.

35. Using the bells for any major scale, create a 16-note melody
and notate it.

36. Using the bells for any minor scale, create a 16-note melody
and play it.

37. Using the bells for any minor scale, create a 16-note melody
and notate it.

38. List any six songs from the music books and indicate if they
are written in major or minor tonalities.

39. On music manuscript paper, write any ten major key signatures and name the keys.

40. On music manuscript paper, write ten minor key signatures
and name the keys.

## Subject: Vertical Sounds

Vertical Sounds in music refers to the study of harmony, chords,
and all matters related thereto. Studying, writing, identifying, naming,

and performing chords and harmonies provide the bulk of these contract
options.

41. Find a friend who will join you in playing a simple round in
two parts on recorders.
42. Work with a friend and sing a simple round in two parts.
43. Use two tape recorders and tape record yourself singing a
simple round in two parts. (Example ''Frère Jacque'')
44. Play any two-chord song on the autoharp.
45. Play any three-chord song on the autoharp.
46. Write and label the I, IV, V, and $V^7$ chords in the key of C.
47. Write and label the I, IV, V, and $V^7$ chords in the key of F.
48. Write and label the I, IV, V, and $V^7$ chords in the key of G.
49. Write the following chords on music manuscript paper: C, F,
G, B♭, D.
50. Write the following chords on music manuscript paper: C,
$C^7$, F, $F^7$, G, $G^7$, B♭, B♭$^7$, D, $D^7$.
51. Play these chords on the piano: D, $D^7$, G, $G^7$, C, $C^7$, F, $F^7$,
B♭. Play each chord twice.
52. Play any two-chord song on the piano.
53. Play any three-chord song on the piano.
54. Play any two-chord song on the guitar.
55. Play any three-chord song on the guitar.
56. Write (in block style) two musical examples of each of the
following intervals: 2nd, 3rd, 4th, 5th, 6th, 7th.
57. Play (on bells or piano) two musical examples of each of the
following intervals: 2nd, 3rd, 4th, 5th, 6th, 7th.
58. Write a tertian chord above each note of the major scale.
59. Play on the piano a tertian chord above each note of the major
scale.
60. Write a tertian chord above each note of the minor scale.
61. Play on the piano a tertian chord above each note of the minor
scale.
62. At the autoharp accompany any two-chord song ''by ear.'
63. At the autoharp accompany any three-chord song ''by ear.''
64. Using music manuscript paper, write six major triads.
65. Using music manuscript paper, write six minor triads.
66. Create on the piano any rock-style rhythms that use this chord
pattern: C, B, F, G.

67. Create on the piano any rock-style rhythms that use this chord pattern: C, A minor, F, G.

## Subject: Techniques Used in Musical Composition

Simple compositional techniques are utilized in the various assignments given here. Repetition, contrast, binary form, ternary form, rondo form, and variations on a theme are among the techniques used. Contract options are also given for the techniques of polyrhythm, polytonality, and atonality, as well as notational devices such as repeat signs, D.C. al fine, and D.S.

68. Write a twelve-note phrase. Repeat the phrase.
69. Play a twelve-note phrase on any pitched instrument. Repeat the phrase.
70. Write two twelve-note melodies. Make them different.
71. Play two twelve-note melodies. Make them different.
72. Play a three-part (ternary) melody which is in A B A form.
73. Create three different twelve-note melodies. Use them in writing a rondo composition: A B A C A.
74. Create and play three different twelve-note melodies. Use them in a rondo composition.
75. Create a sixteen-note melody. Use it to write a theme and two variations.
76. Create and play a sixteen-note melody. Use it to create a theme and two variations in your composition.
77. Using any music textbook (or textbooks), make a list of ten two-part songs.
78. Using any music textbook (or textbooks), make a list of ten songs in ternary (A B A) form.
79. Using an A B A form and any sound-producing materials, create an original A B A sound composition.
80. Using a rondo form and any sound-producing materials, create an original rondo sound composition.
81. Using any music book, list five song titles (and page numbers) that illustrate the following music symbols: repeat signs, D.C. al fine, D.S. repetition, contrast.
82. Create and perform a simple dance which illustrates A B A form. Use any recording suggested by the teacher.

83. Create and perform a simple dance which illustrates a rondo form. Use any recording suggested by the teacher.
84. Create and perform a simple dance which illustrates theme and variation. Use any recording suggested by the teacher.
85. Create and sing an ostinato pattern to accompany the song and singers of your choice.
86. Using the bells of a pentatonic scale, develop and play an ostinato pattern to accompany a song.
87. Play any melody and repeat it using "imitation."
88. Play any melody and repeat it using "variation."
89. Be prepared to point out the main theme or motive in a musical composition. Play the recording for the class; point out the main theme each time that it occurs.
90. Make a drawing which illustrates A B A form.
91. Make a drawing which illustrates rondo form.
92. Make a drawing which illustrates theme and variation.
93. Tape record musical examples of the following: a round and a fugue.
94. Listen to a recording of any theme and variation. How many variations are there? Listen to the recording again; write down something that describes each variation.
95. Tape record musical examples of the following dance forms: waltz, minuet, and gavotte.
96. Tape record four musical examples of an introduction and four musical examples of a coda.
97. Tape record and name musical examples of polyrhythm and polytonality.
98. Tape record any sixteen-note pattern which illustrates atonality in music. Use recordings by Stravinsky, Schoenberg, Bartok, and Ives.
99. Tape record musical examples of the following techniques: polyrhythm, polytonality, and atonality.

## Subject: Music as a Cultural Expression

The music of a country can often reveal much about the culture that exists there. The importance (or lack of it) of home, family, and personal virtues can usually be determined by a survey of song texts. Sophistication and development of the culture can be assessed by surveying the musical instruments being used. The student of culture can learn about a civilization by noting its complexities of rhythm and other musical components.

The following suggested contract projects were designed to aid the student in fostering understanding and concern for all peoples in all times. Do encourage students to create their own assignments; thoughtful student creations may do a great deal in promoting good will everywhere, as well as in fulfilling the aim of teaching music.

100. Listen to recordings of African music; list the characteristics of sounds heard.
101. Listen to recordings of music of the Far East; list the characteristics of sounds heard.
102. Make a list of instruments common to Africa, the Far East, and the United States.
103. Find three examples of African "call and response" music. List or tape record them.
104. Find three examples of African "camp-meeting spirituals." List or tape record them.
105. Tape record a folk song from China or Japan.
106. Tape record a folk song from Hungary.
107. List similarities found in the folk songs of Japan and Hungary.
108. Prepare a demonstration-report on the "steel drum" bands of the Caribbean.
109. Prepare a demonstration-report on any distinctive instrument from any culture.
110. Learn and demonstrate any folk dance.
111. Tape record and name one example of three different styles of jazz: blues, boogie, ragtime, hot, swing, cool, and rock.
112. List ten show titles from American musical theater. With each show title, name one or two songs from that show.
113. List three examples of music from Europe in the nineteenth century.
114. List three examples of music from the United States in the twentieth century.
115. Prepare a report on folk music characteristics (songs and instruments) of any country.
116. Prepare a report on the "History of Jazz."

117.  Prepare a report on "Music in the Church: Now and Then."
118.  Prepare a report on the music performer of your choice.
119.  Prepare a report on the life of the composer of your choice.
120.  Perform any folk music from the country of your choice.
121.  List five movies that have contained one or more songs and list the songs from each movie title.
122.  List and briefly describe the job of all people required to produce an opera.
123.  Prepare a report on the mood or signature music used for the television program of your choice.
124.  Construct an instrument which is patterned after any instrument from another culture.
125.  Prepare a report on the instruments used in modern rock composition.
126.  Create and list an original system for notating natural sound.
127.  Using the words of a rock song, write a report in which you discuss the message of the words as they relate to relationships between people and personal feelings.
128.  Using pictures from your favorite vacation, select background music appropriate to the sequence of pictures. Present your music and pictures to the class.
129.  Make a tape recording which gives (and names) examples of hard rock, soft rock, soul music, and/or other music of today.
130.  Make a drawing which illustrates the styles of clothing associated with the following musical styles: (choose four) African folk music, Hungarian folk music, British rock n' roll, United States ragtime, Japanese folk music, American square dance, and European minuet.

## ANOTHER WAY FOR STUDENTS TO DESIGN MUSIC CONTRACTS

Another way to prepare music contracts is by using a "mix and match" system. In this system a suggested list of contract topics is prepared along with another list which contains appropriate activities. The students simply select a contract topic from List One and match it with an activity from List Two. These lists may be presented by charts on the wall or duplicated in paper booklets for student use. This system has proven to be a delightful device to further motivate and stimulate new ideas among the students.

*Mix-and-Match Music Contracts*

   *Directions:*

   Choose a topic from List #1. Circle your choice. Choose an activity from List #2. Circle your choice. Complete your music contract record sheet. Do the activity as it relates to the topic you selected.

*List #1*

| | |
|---|---|
| The Concert Band | Music for the  (name instrument) |
| The Choir | Musical Theater |
| The Dance | The Orchestra |
| Folk Music | Pop Music |
| Religious Music | History of Music in  (name country) |
| Jazz | Technology in Music |
| The Music Business | Twentieth Century Musical Sounds |

*List #2.*

1. Tape record  (how many)  musical examples of it.
2. Compose and notate  (how many)  examples of it.
3. Create and perform  (how many)  examples of it.
4. Illustrate it with a drawing or picture.
5. Read a book about it.
6. Present an oral report about it. (Read articles for information.)
7. Make a poster about it.
8. List  (how many)  musical titles that represent it.
9. Write a report on a composer who is associated with it.
10. Make a time line that depicts it.

# 8

## Environment-Plus Projects

*I never let schooling interfere with
my education.*

Mark Twain

The whole world is the student's classroom. Teachers must be keenly mindful of incorporating that "whole world" into the learning experience of their students. In bringing the world into the classroom and taking the students into the world, teachers are giving students a deeper acquaintance and understanding of their world and its environment. Learning begins with an experience and continues in a life-long process of exploring the immediate environment. The music teacher who structures experiences in which his students are stimulated by musical situations is truly providing those students with the makings of a superior music education.

## HOW TO DISCOVER A "WORLD" OF MUSIC

The music student who is never required to look about in his home and his community for musical expression and ideas has not received a full measure of educational stimulation. Rather, it is desired that a student's school-music class will prompt him to investigate the family's collection of record albums and to feel an appreciative awareness of his community's brass band as well as the music merchants that help to endow it.

Encouraging students to investigate the functional music of movies or television themes, the Muzak in the shopping center, and the business management of the rock concert can create a genuine interest and appreciation for music; and it might well be best accomplished outside of the music room. Helping students to become acquainted with local performing groups and community music resource persons will cause the student to appreciate music and musicians as part of the "real world."

The Environment-Plus Projects presented in this chapter are designed to make music come alive and become a part of a student's outside-of-music-class life. The bulk of work involved in the Environment-Plus Projects is intended to be done outside of music class. The music class should serve as the catalyst for this educational experience, but the laboratory experience will be staged throughout the school, the homes, the shops, and the entire community. Such experiences should not only serve the cause of music education *in* the school, they should also serve as subtle ambassadors *for* the school in acquainting the community with the school's many-faceted program of music education.

## SCHOOL ASSEMBLY CONCERTS

In developing a well-rounded music education program and a healthy musical environment, the music teacher should give serious consideration to concerts which are presented to the students in the school. Considering that such concerts pre-empt other regularly scheduled classes and school routines, it is imperative that they be both interesting and meaningful. Contributing, as they do, to the total music education of the student, it is imperative that they offer the student a unique concert experience that is stimulating and broadening. The teacher may be well advised to consider each school concert as one of a concert series and to consider variety and quality as each concert is scheduled.

At the first class meeting which follows a school assembly concert, take a minute to mention the concert experience to your class. You may find it helpful to make notes to yourself immediately following the concert, noting things that might be mentioned later in the music class. Here, also, is an opportunity to remind students that letters of appreciation to guest performers are a courteous and gracious gesture.

Presenting an award for good audience behavior is highly motivating as you teach "how to be an audience." All levels of students love the large gold medallion with red velvet streamers that secretly appears in the music room the day following a concert where the audience was "superior."

## Possibilities for School Assembly Concerts

- Community choirs, bands, orchestras
- Community dance ensembles
- Performing groups from nearby colleges and universities
- Performing groups from the local high school
- Performing groups from a local junior high or middle school
- Performing groups from a neighboring elementary or middle school
- Quartets from the local chapter, Society for Preservation and Encouragement of Barbershop Quartet Singing in America or the Sweet Adelines
- Local folk music groups
- Local rock music groups
- Soloists from the community
- Performing groups from ethnic culture clubs
- Local disc jockey
- Lecturers of musical skills
- Craftsmen
- Young Audience Inc. Programs or similar groups

Seek out the type of performing groups that you want in your school and invite them to come. Invite them early, and you might find them eager to perform for you. If the scheduled performing group is not affiliated with a school, it is wise to check in advance to see if a fee is expected. If there is a fee involved, appeal to your school's organization of parents. Parent organizations have been known to provide thousands of schools with experiences that would have been otherwise impossible.

After scheduling the school assembly concert, publicize it with student-made posters in the hallways, an item in the school-community newsletter, or perhaps an announcement flier that is sent into every home. The school patrons love to know of special events at school, and some parents may want to attend.

## FIELD TRIPS

Trips away from the school and into the "real world" can help to make students more vividly aware of musical elements in the total environment. Therefore, it is desirable that the music teacher plan music class field trips regularly. "Regularly" may range from monthly to bi-annually, depending on the circumstances. For Ms. Holmes in her suburban school, an annual field trip for each grade level was the best solution. She perfected a field trip planning list which proved a valuable aid in saving time.

The field trip planning list reminded her to:

1. Clear the field trip date with the school office.
2. Arrange with host for the class's visit.
3. Arrange students' transportation.
4. Provide parents with letters of information about the trip, including what, when, where, why, how, and how much.
5. Provide students with forms to be signed and returned to the school.
6. Arrange for parent escorts.
7. Determine if other school faculty will make the trip with you.
8. Determine if any special lunch arrangements will be needed for the group.
9. Arrange for any conflicts that would result from the music teacher's being away from school.
10. Be sure that the school principal is acquainted with all the plans.

In preparation for the field trip, Ms. Holmes attempted to inform her class, as completely as possible, of exactly what they would experience. She wanted them to know what specific things to observe; sometimes she would assign specific questions to be answered. Also, she would remind the students to be on their best behavior. Through the use of this approach, Ms. Holmes was usually not disappointed, and the students were always eager for their annual field trip.

Following the field trip, the class should be given an opportunity to react verbally to the field trip experience. There are several ways of providing such opportunities.

- Ask the students to write a paragraph outlining what they observed or experienced.
- Provide several questions for students to answer on paper.
- Ask each student to tell one thing he observed.
- Lead the students in a discussion of the field trip experience.

In assessing the field trip, it is important that the teacher help the students to realize that the value of the trip lies in its providing a unique and new experience rather than in the student's personal enjoyment. Did the trip provide a new and/or unique experience? If the answer is absolutely affirmative, then you may want to repeat the trip with a different music class.

Some suggested field trip experiences

- See a pipe organ demonstration.
- See a synthesizer demonstration.
- Attend a concert.
- Attend a ballet.
- Attend a rehearsal of a professional performing group.
- Visit a museum or gallery.
- See a demonstration of instruments.
- Tour a recording studio.
- Tour a broadcasting studio.
- Tour an instrument factory.
- Visit a music dealer and tour the music store.
- Attend a musical event at the local high school.

## GUEST SPEAKERS

Nothing brightens the day anywhere like having guests; and music class is no exception. Furthermore, people offer the epitome of cultural resources. So, in searching for ways to incorporate the cultural environment with that of the classroom, people are the logical resource with which to begin. Let the students know that a guest is expected, and let them know the purpose of the visit so that they can share your anticipation of the visit. Have a student act as a special greeter and host for the guest. If possible, allow a student to introduce the guest and host the presentation to the class.

Following the presentation, allow some time for questions and discussions. Let the students know how they may pursue the subject further and then ask a student to escort the guest to the door. Be sure that you and the students promptly send letters of appreciation to the guest. Such courtesies must never be ignored!

## Card File of Community Resource People

Your school may have a card file of community resource people who would be valuable as guest speakers for music class. Research the card file and glean from it all possibilities. Add to it (or begin a separate file) all additional possibilities that you are able to unearth.

The best way to begin discovering resource people is by surveying your students. Have them indicate if their parents or friends can offer a musical contribution to the class. You might use a form similar to the one in Figure 23 to survey your students. Update your card file early in September and use it all year.

---

### STUDENT SURVEY FORM
### OF COMMUNITY RESOURCE PEOPLE

Student's Name _____

Father's Name _____

    Is music one of his hobbies? (yes or no) _____

    If yes, describe how: _____

Mother's Name _____

    Is music one of her hobbies? (yes or no) _____

    If yes describe how: _____

Are you acquainted with anyone (including your family)
    who would be a good guest speaker for music class?
    If so, please list their:

      Name _____

      Telephone Number _____

      What could they share with our class? _____

---

**Figure 23**

By using the school's card file, Mrs. Norton managed to secure an expert violin-maker for a visit to her music class. By surveying the students she discovered and invited a mother who demonstrated and played the dulcimer as well as a father who discussed and performed the piano music of Debussy. By being alert to news stories, Mrs. Norton learned of a Mexican mariachi band which was appearing at a nearby shopping center. After several telephone calls, she was ultimately rewarded by having two of the band members visit her music class. The visit provided a rich and meaningful experience for the class.

The students also helped in securing guest speakers for the music class. Through the years, Mrs. Norton could recall having presentations made by visiting grandmothers, grandfathers, aunts, uncles, big brothers, big sisters, or friends. The topics of the presentations ranged from "Playing in a Rock Band" to "Synchronizing Music with Animated Cartoons," and the quality of the presentations ran the gamut from excellent to poor. But there was never a student who failed to be proud of "his" special-guest relative or friend. And because the guests came from one of their own classmate's families, the students were always gracious.

### Possible Guest Speakers:

- Music performers of all kinds
- Music composers
- Music arrangers, directors, producers
- Music merchants
- Music manufacturers
- Music teachers of all kinds (pre-school to college)
- Music journalists (critics/editors)
- Music consultants for television/radio programs
- Music printers
- Music publishers
- Sound recording technicians
- Disc jockeys
- Sound/Acoustical experts
- Instrument builders
- Instrument repairmen
- Piano tuners
- Dance experts

## PROJECTS FOR THE INDIVIDUAL STUDENT

Students must be encouraged to glean musical experiences from their cultural environment. They cannot be expected to see unless they are made aware of the opportunities abounding in their surroundings. They must be motivated and encouraged to capture some of its richness for their own. In attempting to accomplish these things, Mr. Conrad required every student to accomplish at least one Environment-Plus Project during each semester. Each project was designed to be accomplished completely outside of music class and with the utilization of environmental effects such as books, recordings, and the news media. Students were advised of the requirement early in the semester, and success in fulfilling the requirement became part of the regular report to the parents.

Mr. Conrad gave occasional reminders of the assignment. He regularly mentioned upcoming musical events in the community or on television; and, to make it even more emphatic (and easy for the student!), he carefully incorporated one of the Environment-Plus Project assignments into each semester's course of study. This was accomplished in a meeting with the entire class by announcing and discussing the specific assignment, designating a reasonable deadline date, and emphasizing that the work should be done outside of music class. Mr. Conrad developed a distinctive assignment for each of four semesters so that the continuing student would have a new Environment-Plus Project assignment each term.

| *Term* | *Environment-Plus Project Assignment* |
| --- | --- |
| Grade 5, first semester | Construct and demonstrate a homemade musical instrument |
| Grade 5, second semester | Attend a concert and complete an individual project report form (Figure 24) |
| Grade 6, first semester | View an assigned movie or television program and complete an individual project report form. |
| Grade 6, second semester | Environment-Plus Project of student's choice |

Any student who preferred to choose an alternate project was encouraged to do so. Primarily, the objective was to get each student

ENVIRONMENT-PLUS INDIVIDUAL PROJECT
REPORT FORM

Student's Name _____
Grade/Homeroom _____
Date _____

Directions: Circle the appropriate *number* and complete that line.

1. I read a BOOK. It contained _____ pages.
   (how many)

2. I attended a CONCERT. It was presented at the
   _____ .
   (name of place)

3. I viewed a MOVIE. It was shown at
   _____ .
   (name of place)

4. I viewed a TELEVISION PROGRAM. It was shown
   _____ , _____ .
   (date,      time,      channel)

5. I took a MUSIC TOUR. I went on _____
   (date)

   with _____ .
   (what others)

Complete the following:
Name of Book, Concert, Movie, TV program or Music Tour:
_____
_____
Author, Main Performer, or Host: _____
Write a short description of the Book, Performance or Place.
_____
_____
_____
_____
_____
_____

Did you enjoy this experience? _____
_____
_____
_____

**Figure 24**

involved in at least one Environment-Plus Project each semester. The teacher avoided any project assignments that required student performance of music. The program was designed for *all* students to utilize their environment plus their ingenuity.

## Ten Suggested Environment-Plus Projects for Individuals

(One project is required per semester. Each specific project must be approved by the teacher.)

1. Read a book about music or musicians; complete the individual project report form.
2. Attend a concert; complete the individual project report form.
3. View a movie about a musician or music; complete an individual project report form.
4. View a television program about music or musicians; complete the individual project report form.
5. Tour a musical place of your choice; complete the individual project report form.
6. Construct a homemade musical instrument; demonstrate it at school.
7. List a family record collection of at least 12 albums. Give the list to your teacher.
8. Invite a guest speaker to music class. Arrange it with the teacher.
9. Prepare a "Music in the News" bulletin board of at least six clippings.
10. Write a thank-you letter to a guest performer or guest speaker who came to school. Give the letter to your teacher.

## Student Choice Projects

During the second semester of grade six, Mrs. Morgan offered her students the opportunity to select their own Environment-Plus Project. She announced a deadline date, re-emphasized that Environment-Plus Projects should be accomplished outside of music class, and offered a list of 25 possible projects from which to choose. Each of the 25 suggestions resulted in some student-made product that could be shared with the class. The sharing of those completed projects consumed about two full music classes, and it provided fun and satisfaction for the teacher and her students.

## TWENTY-FIVE ENVIRONMENT-PLUS
## PROJECTS FOR STUDENT CHOICE

Directions: Complete any of the following projects. Have it ready by the deadline date. Be prepared to share your finished project with the class.

1. Make a tape recording of "Environmental Sounds" (wind, rain, household sounds, outdoor sounds, any "natural" sounds).
2. Tape record and identify bird songs.
3. Tape record "Musical Examples that Convey a Definite Theme," such as peace, war, struggle, love, and so on.
4. Tape record examples which represent "The Music of a City."
5. Tape record yourself reading "An Original Story with an Improvised Overture." Use any desired musical sounds for the overture, but the overture should be related to the story.
6. Interview a professional musician about his work. Prepare a report on the interview. The report may be written or tape recorded.
7. Make a diorama to depict any event in recent or ancient music history.
8. Make a drawing or illustration depicting any event in recent or ancient music history.
9. Write and present a play depicting any event in recent or ancient music history.
10. Practice and demonstrate how you would conduct a specific orchestral recording.
11. Form a band or choral group; make a tape recording of your group.
12. Present a dance that you choreographed with your choice of musical recording.
13. Share a collection of antique sheet music or music books.
14. Share a collection of any music-related objects such as concert programs, composer's pictures, performers pictures, specific recordings, books about music, and so on.
15. Organize and take a field trip to a local music store or other place that deals with musical instruments (for example, a repair shop or a factory).

16. Bake cookies that are cut in shapes of music notes/symbols.
17. Design and/or create a new musical instrument.
18. Make advertisements for a musical product.
19. Prepare a "Career Report" on any musical occupation.
20. Write a news story as if (a certain event in music history) had just happened.
21. Make and share a music scrapbook of newspaper/magazine clippings.
22. Prepare a report about antique music boxes or record players.
23. Make a newspaper featuring musical news of your school.
24. Prepare a report about antique musical instruments.
25. Draw a cartoon strip to tell a music story.

## MUSIC AWARDS PROGRAM

To provide motivation and reward for students who desire to do more than the one required Environment-Plus Project per semester, you may want to establish a music awards program. In this program the student selects as desired from a list of Environment-Plus Projects for a Music Award. The actual music award may take the form of a badge or certificate; it is designed to recognize outstanding performance and diligence in the study of music. The awards can be presented at any appropriate ceremony near the end of the school year. Programs of music awards have proven successful and meaningful to many student participants.

### Music Award Requirements

To earn a music award the student must, within a school year, complete any six projects from the List of Environment-Plus Projects for a music award. All projects are designed to integrate the outside-of-music-class cultural environment of books, films, and so on with the human element of intelligence and interpretation. The music awards program is designed so that both the highly motivated non-performing student and the gifted performing student will find it appealing, challenging, and yet within the scope of his personal accomplishments. Further, the element of service to the school and community has been considered in designing many of the suggested projects. Music is an art to be shared; teachers have a responsibility to encourage sharing beyond the classroom and to recognize and commend it.

*Twenty-Five Environment-Plus*
*Projects for a Music Award*

Completion of six of these projects during the school year will entitle the student to a music award. Any project may be completed two times. All projects are subject to the teacher's approval.

1.  Read a book about music or musicians and completed the individual project report form.
2.  Attended a concert and completed the individual project report form.
3.  Viewed a movie about music or musicians and completed the individual project report form.
4.  Viewed a television program about music or musicians and completed the individual project report form.
5.  Took any musical tour and completed the individual project report form.
6.  Constructed a homemade musical instrument and demonstrated it.
7.  Listed a family record collection of at least 12 albums.
8.  Invited a guest speaker to music class and arranged it with the teacher.
9.  Prepared a "Music in the News" bulletin board of at least six clippings.
10.  Wrote a thank-you letter to a guest performer or guest speaker who came to school.
11.  Completed Music Merit Badge for Scouts (or similar organization).
12.  Completed six months participation in a church or temple choir.
13.  Performed with a community band or orchestra (previous summer counts here).
14.  Performed with a community choir. (previous summer counts here).
15.  Performed with a community musical theater (previous summer counts here).
16.  Completed six months of private music or dance lessons.
17.  Performed in a recital of private music or dance teacher.
18.  Participated for seven months in school band or orchestra (including attendance at concerts).

19. Participated for seven months in school choir (including attendance at concerts).
20. Served for seven months as attendance clerk or librarian for school band, orchestra, or choir.
21. Served for seven months as a cadet to help the music teacher with chairs, risers, or music stands.
22. Designed program covers for a school concert.
23. Played piano accompaniment for at least one song at a choir concert.
24. Played wind instrument, string instrument, mallet instrument, or snare drum accompaniment for at least one song at a choir concert.
25. Participated in any musical performance for a school talent show.

The teacher may find it desirable to have students "enlist" early in the school year if they intend to work for a music award and to keep a file folder for each student who has enlisted. In the folder all Individual Project Report Forms and other evidences of each project's completion can be kept. The requirements for earning the music award should be altered as circumstances warrant.

# 9

## Musical Stories, Puzzles, Games, and Activities for the "Fringes of Time"

*All things are difficult before they are easy.*

Thomas Fuller

Did your ever pause to consider the moments in the school day of your students when they have "fringes of time"? Such moments occur when they are walking through the hallways, when they are waiting outside the music room for class, and during the silent visual learning that occurs in a regular music class from stimuli within the room. Such idle moments may be healthy, but they also provide golden teaching opportunities.

In Mrs. Remington's music room she made a Composer Corner which featured a different composer each month. She never mentioned the display; the students never mentioned the display; it was simply there. After a few months, Mrs. Remington removed the Composer Corner and was amazed at the students' response to its absence. She discovered that they remembered every composer that had been featured; some students even speculated about which composer would appear next.

You might enjoy developing a Composer Corner before taking advantage of other places in the room where displays might fill somebody's "fringes of time." These displays do not need to be elaborate or spectacular. A simple paper containing "A Curious Question" can create much student interest when the answer is written on the back side of the paper. Another successful idea is writing "Secret Messages" on the chalkboard, using musical notation when possible. Familiar tunes can quickly become "Mystery Tunes" when you notate them on large manuscript paper and post them on the back of the piano. Your students will love to look at this for "clues" in identifying the tune.

Another often-overlooked place is the doorway to your music room. You might place a box or large envelope of music puzzle papers like those found later in this chapter near the doorway. Simply label them "Take-Home Teasers." Another time, perhaps, a typical hallway bulletin board can become an Action Bulletin Board when it is used for a series of displays entitled "Have You Heard?" Students enjoy changing and maintaining the various musical displays.

In addition to regular activities in the music class, students can absorb a great deal of musical knowledge in their "fringes of time." To certain students, the appeal of these "incidental learnings" becomes the chief reason for extra visits to the music room.

## BRAIN STIMULATORS FOR INSIDE THE MUSIC ROOM

### Be Sharp!

Make a small poster with the permanent headline, "Be Sharp!"

Perhaps a card which bears a single question in the beak of the parrot. Write the answer on the reverse side of the card. Simply hook the card to the bill with a paper clip. Display the poster beside the pencil sharpener. Change the questions weekly and save the question cards to use another year.

Suggested items for "Be Sharp" poster:

1. Can you name five composers whose last names begin with "B"? (Bach, Brahms, Beethoven, Bernstein, Bacharach)
2. Can you name two composers whose names begin with the letter "H"? (Handel, Haydn)
3. Can you name the composer of _____? (_____)
4. How many letters are used in the music alphabet? (Seven: A B C D E F G)
5. What is the difference between a concert band and an orchestra? (A band has no stringed instruments.)
6. Can you name five different ways in which musicians may find full-time jobs? (composer, conductor, performer, school teacher, merchant, studio teacher, television advisor, salesman)
7. What is the name of the stand a conductor stands on while conducting? (podium)
8. In music, what is the meaning of the word "score"? (the printed music manuscript)
9. What is the term given to orchestral music which depicts a story? (program music)
10. What is a musical suite? (a group of pieces that go together)

### Musical Chalk Talk

Designate a section of the chalk board to be used for Musical Chalk Talk. If your chalk board space is limited, use chalk to write on black art paper which has been sprayed with hair spray, and you have a good facsimile of an old-fashioned blackboard. The paper-board has an advantage in that it can be stored and used another year. Change the display every week or so.

Suggested items for Musical Chalk Talk:

Each item is a question with the answer written in music notation.

1. What did the younger generation say about the older generation?

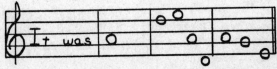

2.  What is another name for a cattle barn?

    A  B E E F   C A G E

3.  What did the carrot shout to the cole slaw?

    Hello,   C A B B A G E   F A C E

4.  How might you describe an infant with an empty bottle?

    A  F E D   B A B E

5.  How did the Mother Hen explain her naughty chick?

    A  B A D   E G G

6.  What did Yogi Bear find in the honey?

    A  D E A D   B E E

7.  Describe the father of the bride on the day after the wedding?

    A  F A D E D   D A D

8.  How did the lady know that her purse was made by Indians?

    It was  A  B E A D E D   B A G

9.  What did the Boy Scout say was in his backpack?

    A  B A G G E D   B E D

10.  What happened when Ed got a pie in his face?

    A  D E F A C E D   E D

11.  How much salt is required to make one cake?

    A  D A B

12.  Why was the old man unable to use his telephone?

    He was  D E A F

13.  Why did the victim of the robbery not call the police?

    He was  G A G G E D

14.  How did the boy win the poker game?

    With an  A C E

15.  How did the kid carry the groceries home?

    In  A  B A G

## Composer Circles

Choose an area your students often pass in which to hang Composer Circles. The students will be delighted with this fascinating learning device.

*Procedure:*

Cut two large circles. In Circle A cut a wedge-shaped window like this:

Also on Circle A, just above the window, print the words, "Did you know?" Opposite the window, print the name of a composer in large letters.

On Circle B you need to place factual statements about the composer that can be revealed in the window of the smaller circle. To make the statements "fit," you may need to type the statements and then cut and paste them to Circle B.

After placing ten or so statements in a "wheel" design on the Circle B, place Circle A on top of Circle B and attach the circles, using a metal fastener in the center. Circle A can then be turned so that its window reveals each fact one at a time.

Change Composer Circles every few weeks. Save them for another year.

CIRCLE A        CIRCLE B

## Music Math

Use an area of the chalkboard or a poster to display problems in Music Math. One or two problems will be enough for each display. Just change them often and see what attention they attract.

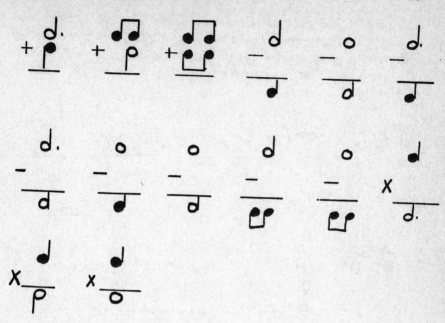

## Music Stories

All underlined words should appear as music notation.

### Ed's Work

ED picked up his BAGGAGE and headed for the old shed. It was an AGED place—more like a CAGE for animals than a home for people. ED touched his BADGE as he knocked. A small BABE was playing on the porch; the BAG of CABBAGE lay nearby. ED opened the door and went in.

### Ada's Work

ADA opened a BEAD shop. She thought it was a FAD that might pay off. Many people visited the shop. Some came to BEG; some came to DEFACE the doorway; hardly anyone came to buy a BEAD. ADA decided to FACE the truth and admit that a BEAD shop was not successful. So, she closed the BEAD shop and opened an EGG shop instead.

## Music in the News

Cut the letters for this headline from the classified ads of the newspaper. In the space under the headline, post any news articles about musicals, music, or musical events. Many Sunday newspapers are a good source of such clippings, as are magazines such as *Time* and *Newsweek*. Don't forget to keep this display area current, and do solicit student contributions.

**Figure 25**

*Instrument Investigator*

    Near the top of a large piece of poster board, place the words

"Instrument Investigator." Also on the poster, place two cartoon-type characters (draw them or cut and paste). One of the characters should appear to be asking a question, and the other character should appear to be answering (Figure 25). Draw a large "word balloon" from each character's mouth. Use these "word balloon" spaces to display the questions and answers which make the substance of this poster. Attach the question and answer cards with loops of tape (or make a small diagonal cut in the poster to hold the card corners). Save the poster to use another year. The questions should all concern musical instruments

Suggestions for Instrument Investigator:

Print the answer on one card and the question on another.

1.  What is another name for an acoustic guitar? (folk guitar)
2.  How many keys are on a piano? (88)
3.  What instrument is sometimes called a "licorice stick"? (clarinet)
4.  How many strings are on a ukulele? (four)
5.  How many strings are on a cello? (four)
6.  How many valves are on a trumpet? (three)
7.  What brass instrument is fingered with the left hand? (French horn)
8.  What instrument is made of brass, but played with a reed and classified as "woodwind"? (saxophone)
9.  What do pianos and accordions have in common? (keyboard)
10. Name a double-reed instrument that plays high sounds. (oboe)
11. What instrument is usually the most numerous in an orchestra? (violin)
12. What instrument is usually the most numerous in a band? (clarinet)
13. What instrument sounds like a tuba but is more convenient to use in a marching band? (sousaphone)
14. What brass instrument produces the highest sounds? (trumpet)
15. Name two categories that all percussion instruments fit into. (melodic and non-melodic)

## Musical Maps

Display an outline of a nation. On the map write the name of the nation and several distinctive features of the nation's folk music. Decorate each map with appropriate magazine pictures. Display a different map each month.

*United States Folk Music*

Songs about:     building railroads
                 picking cotton
                 settling the West
                 cowboys

Instruments:     banjos
                 guitars
                 harmonicas

Musical characteristics:     simple harmonies
                             steady rhythms

*Latin American Folk Music*

Songs about:     fiestas
                 dark-eyed ladies

Instruments:     string instruments
                 brass instruments
                 percussion

Musical characteristics:     complicated rhythms
                             simple harmonies
                             instrumental refrains

*German Folk Music*

Songs about:     love of homeland and family
                 ballads

Instruments:     accordion
                 clarinet

Musical characteristics:     steady beats
                             major keys
                             triadic melodies and harmonies

*African Folk Music*

Songs about:     ceremonies
                 the work
                 the weather

Instruments:     drums
                 rattles

xylophones
musical bow
thumb piano (mbira)
Musical characteristics: complicated rhythms
solo-chorus vocal performances
solo improvisations

*South Pacific Islands Folk Music*

Songs about: warfare
dancing
homeland
Instruments: ukuleles
drums
bamboo sticks (puili)
Musical characterisitics: strict rhythms
chant-like melodies
simple harmonies

*British Isles Folk Music*

Songs about: ballads of love
ballads of historical incidents
nonsense syllables
Instruments: dulcimers
fiddles
bagpipes
Musical characteristics: steady rhythms
major modes

*Russian Folk Music*

Songs about: heroes
sweethearts
battles
Instruments: balalaikas
domras
tambourines
Musical characteristics: minor modes
simple harmonies
lilting melodies

*Spanish Folk Music*

Songs about:   heroes
                    senoritas
                    bullfights

Instruments:   guitars
                    castanets

Musical characteristics:   flamenco rhythms
                                         triple meter
                                         major-minor modes

*Japanese Folk Music*

Songs about:   happiness
                    beauty
                    lovely things

Instruments:   koto
                    bamboo flute

Musical characteristics:   pentatonic scale system
                                         duple rhythms

*American Indian Folk Music*

Songs about:   weather
                    love
                    ceremonies

Instruments:   drum/rattle
                    flute

Musical characteristics:   strong rhythms
                                         song accompanies dance
                                         ceremonial song-dance tells story

## BRAIN STIMULATORS FOR OUTSIDE THE MUSIC ROOM: ACTION BULLETIN BOARDS

Adopt a bulletin board in the hallway outside the music room. Make a new display for it each month. Using teacher-aides or parent volunteers or students makes this job easier. Design the displays so that they require the observer to respond in some way. Involve the student in moving things, matching things, categorizing things, naming things, or ordering a set of things.

Provide push-pins, thumb tacks, magnetic figures, or flannel figures for the student observers to use. Suggest that after completing the display, the student may "set it up" again for another student to complete. Always provide a self-checking answer paper that is hidden below, beneath, behind, or someplace near the display.

Several suggestions for Action Bulletin Boards are given in this chapter. Place the headline for each bulletin board at the top of the display. Write the headline on a strip of oak tag or use ready-made letters from a school-supply house. Then follow directions as given. Do try all of the ideas; adapt them; change them; invent your own; and just see what a stir can be created by these magical pieces of musical learnings!

## To Which Family Does Each Instrument Belong?

Under the headline, list the four instrument families: String, Woodwind, Brass, and Percussion. Beside each family's name, indicate its color-code for this display. Beneath the instrument families list as many orchestral instruments as desired. Make available as many push-pins as there are instruments listed. The push-pins should be color-coded to match the instrument family names listed. The idea is for the student to push a pin of the appropriate color beside each instrument listed.

---

**TO WHICH FAMILY DOES EACH INSTRUMENT BELONG?**

| String: | Percussion: |
|---|---|
| Woodwind: | Brass: |

| | |
|---|---|
| Cello | Trumpet |
| Flute | Violin |
| Snare drum | Clarinet |
| Trombone | Oboe |
| Cymbal | Viola |
| French horn | Piccolo |
| Harp | Tuba |

---

## Arrange These Notes from Shortest to Longest Sounds

Place the headline at the top of the bulletin board. Beneath the headline tack a square of flannel. On the flannel, randomly place four flannel-backed notes: whole, half, quarter, and eighth. The idea is for the student to arrange the notes in the required order.

```
┌─────────────────────────────────────────────────┐
│  ARRANGE THESE NOTES FROM SHORTEST TO LONGEST    │
│                                                  │
│              ♪   o   ♩   ♩                        │
│                                                  │
└─────────────────────────────────────────────────┘
```

### *Arrange These Terms from Softest to Loudest*

Beneath the headline, tack a felt square. On the square, in random order, place six terms: Pianissimo, Piano, Mezzo Piano, Mezzo Forte, Forte, Fortissimo. The idea is for students to arrange the terms in the required order.

```
┌───────────────────────────────────────────────────┐
│                                                   │
│    ARRANGE THESE TERMS FROM SOFTEST TO LOUDEST    │
│                                                   │
│              ┌─────────────────┐                  │
│              │ Piano           │                  │
│              │ Mezzo Forte     │                  │
│              │ Forte           │                  │
│              │ Mezzo Piano     │                  │
│              │ Pianissimo      │                  │
│              │ Fortissimo      │                  │
│              └─────────────────┘                  │
│                                                   │
└───────────────────────────────────────────────────┘
```

### *Arrange the Instruments from Highest to Lowest*

Beneath the headline, tack a felt square. On the square place names or pictures of several musical instruments in random order. The idea is for students to arrange the instruments in the order of their pitch.

```
┌───────────────────────────────────────────────────┐
│              ARRANGE THE INSTRUMENTS              │
│               FROM HIGHEST TO LOWEST              │
│                                                   │
│              ┌─────────────────┐                  │
│              │ Contra bassoon   │                 │
│              │ Piccolo          │                 │
│              │ Trombone         │                 │
│              │ Flute            │                 │
│              │ Trumpet          │                 │
│              └─────────────────┘                  │
│                                                   │
└───────────────────────────────────────────────────┘
```

## Can You Name Keyboard Instruments?

Beneath the headline, display a picture of several of these: piano, pipe organ, accordion, synthesizer, celeste, melodica, electric piano, electric organ. Beside each picture, place a number. The idea is for the student to name each instrument that is pictured. The answer-check can code the answer with their picture numbers.

---

### CAN YOU NAME KEYBOARD INSTRUMENTS?

| 1. Pipe Organ Picture | 2. Piano Picture |
|---|---|
| 3. Accordion Picture | 4. Melodica Picture |
| 5. Synthesizer Picture | 6. Celeste Picture |

---

## Which Voice Is the Right Voice?

Beneath the headline, list the words: Soprano, Alto, Tenor, and Bass. Beside each of the voices listed, place a small patch of flannel or felt. Near the bottom of the display, place a rectangle of flannel or felt. Arrange the flannel-backed cards randomly on the rectangle. The cards may say: "high female voice," "low female voice," "high male voice," and "low male voice." The idea is for the students to match the voice with its definition

---

### WHICH VOICE IS THE RIGHT VOICE?

Soprano ☐
Alto ☐
Tenor ☐
Bass ☐

| low male voice | high female voice |
|---|---|
| low female voice | high male voice |

## Match the Music Symbol with Its Name

Beneath the headline, list the names of several music symbols such as treble clef, bass clef, repeat sign, and so on. Beside each name, place a patch of flannel or felt. Near the bottom of the display, hang an open envelope which contains all necessary flannel-backed symbols. The idea is for the student to match the symbol with its name.

---

### MATCH THE MUSIC SYMBOL WITH ITS NAME

| | | |
|---|---|---|
| Treble Clef ☐ | Repeat ☐ | Quarter note ☐ |
| Fermata ☐ | Bass Clef ☐ | Staff ☐ |
| Sharp ☐ | Flat ☐ | Half note ☐ |

Symbols

---

## What Nation Was My Home?

Under the headline, list (in color code) several nations such as England, Germany, Italy, and the United States. Below the list of nations, post the names of composers—as many as you wish. Make colored push-pins available. The idea is that the student will place a pin of the appropriate color beside the name of each composer.

---

### WHAT NATION WAS MY HOME?

| | | |
|---|---|---|
| England: ♪♪ | Italy: ♪♪ | France: ♪♪ |
| Germany: ♪♪ | United States: ♪♪ | Russia: ♪♪ |

| | | | |
|---|---|---|---|
| Bach | MacDowell | Strauss | Ives |
| Wagner | Beethoven | Brahms | Debussy |
| Sousa | Tchaikovsky | Handel | Puccini |

---

## Can You Find a Mistake Here?

Use black yarn and a stapler to construct a music staff prominently in the center of this display. On the staff place a clef sign, a meter sign, and a key signature. (Use your flannel-graph symbols and attach them with staples or small loops of tape.) Notate a four-measure musical phrase on the staff, complete with melody, rhythm, barlines, and one deliberate mistake (such as incorrect number of beats in one measure or incorrect key signature). Near the bottom of the display, make available a sturdy cardboard arrow and thumb tack. The student is supposed to place the arrow so that it points to the mistake.

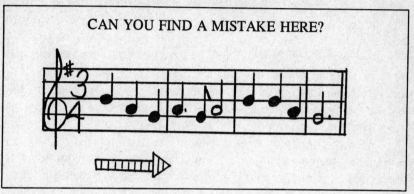

CAN YOU FIND A MISTAKE HERE?

### Place the Missing Barlines

Use black yarn and a stapler to construct a music staff prominently in the center of this display. On the staff place a clef sign, a meter sign, and a key signature. Notate a four-measure phrase on the staff, but do not include barlines except at the end. Near the bottom of the display, place three pieces of yarn or felt which may be used as barlines. The idea is for the student to place the barlines in their proper places. The yarn or felt provided should adhere to the yarn staff without other aids, but straight pins or push-pins may be provided.

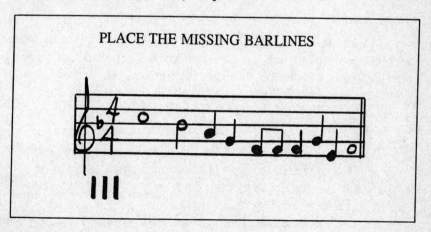

PLACE THE MISSING BARLINES

## EXPERIENCE CENTERS FOR ANYTIME

Try to find some small nook or cranny in your classroom that can become an Experience Center—a place where a student may while away some "fringes of time" by making some "quickie" musical discoveries. Experience Centers may also be successfully placed in the school's media center or some other central location away from the music room.

An Experience Center should be strictly "hands-on" experiences; and the students should respond to its stimuli by touching, handling, feeling, or strumming the objects of learning. The Experience Center can be simply a small table or student desk with a card attached which says "Experience Center" or "Try This." On the table may be placed the "object" of learning with or without directions taped to the tabletop. No record-keeping or other accountability should be required of the Experience Center. Keep it completely open and free of rules; require only consideration of other people and consideration of the equipment.

### Using an Instrument at the Experience Center

Place a xylophone at the Experience Center. An autoharp, ukulele, guitar, or one of the Orff-type instruments may also appear there. Instrument Task Cards may or may not be made available —whatever best suits your particular purpose. It may be desirable to post a chart showing the fingering of chords or melodies nearby. The main purpose is to make an instrument available for a student to experience during his "fringes of time."

### Using Sound Cylinders at the Experience Center

Place Sound Cylinders (several matched pairs of closed cylinders that contain sound materials such as rice, pebbles, noodles, and so on) at the Experience Center. Let the exploring student shake each cylinder to discover the matched pairs. Watch aural discrimination in action!

### Using the Sense of Touch at the Experience Center

Place several flannel-graph music symbols in a covered box with only a side opening for the hand. Let the exploring student put a hand into the box and attempt to identify the music symbol that he grasps. It proves to be an interesting challenge!

Prepare some cards by gluing some music symbols made of sandpaper or different fabrics. The student can search with his hands for a matching pair.

## Using the Flannelboard at the Experience Center

Place a staff, key signature, and meter sign on the music flannelboard. Provide an assortment of notes for the student to use in constructing a melody. It should be in accordance with the key and meter given.

## Visual Discrimination at the Experience Center

- Place two sets of Note Cards (each card contains a drawing of a staff, clef sign, and one note) at the Experience Center. Let the student search for matching pairs of notes. Working to do this quickly can be a beneficial experience to the music student at any level of learning.
- Place Instrument Puzzles (made from large pictures of instruments which have been cut into various shapes) at the Experience Center. For a real challenge, work against the clock and leave a message to the next challenger with your time.
- Place Composer Picture Puzzles (made from large pictures of composers which have been cut into various shapes) at the Experience Center. This is a good challenge against the clock.
- Make a collage of pictures of instruments. Try to locate specific instruments as quickly as you can. The choice of instruments can be from a deck of Instrument Playing Cards (cards with names of instruments on them).

## TAKE-HOME TEASERS

Hang a large manila envelope labeled "Take-Home Teasers" near the exit of the music room. In the envelope place multiple copies of musical games such as Hidden Words, Crossword Puzzles, Scrambled Words, and Musical Stories with notated words. Use only one "teaser" at a time; change the "teaser" regularly and always keep it optional.

Some students will be especially eager to master every word game—and some students will become quite adept at creating new ones.

## Folk Instruments: Scrambled Words

Find the following words in the list below: accordion, autoharp, banjo, dulcimer, fiddle, guitar, harmonica, jaw harp, mandolin, mouthbow, saw, spoons, tub bass, ukulele.

1. trugia   (guitar)
2. joanb   (banjo)
3. loanndim   (mandolin)
4. roocacind   (accordion)
5. diefld   (fiddle)
6. cudilrem   (dulcimer)
7. aphotaru   (autoharp)
8. lukeelu   (ukulele)
9. onopss   (spoons)
10. aws   (saw)
11. stabbsu   (tub bass)
12. raamichon   (harmonica)
13. phawrja   (jaw harp)
14. twohobum   (mouthbow)

## Music in Concert: Scrambled Words

Find these words in the list below: audience, band, cantata, chorus, concerto, conductor, encore, opera, operetta, orchestra, overture, program, soloist, symphony, usher.

1. preoa   (opera)
2. reotapet   (operetta)
3. hersu   (usher)
4. actanta   (cantata)
5. psoyhnym   (symphony)
6. reenoc   (encore)
7. roetevru   (overture)
8. loostis   (soloist)
9. netoorcc   (concerto)
10. cedunaie   (audience)
11. magprro   (program)
12. shucro   (chorus)
13. asothrecr   (orchestra)
14. nadb   (band)
15. trococund   (conductor)

## Music Symbol: Dot to Dot

Follow the numbers to discover a "secret" music symbol.

9*

10*

8*

11*

7*        12*

13*

14*        6*

15*        24*            23*

25*        5*            22*

16*

26*        4*            21*

17*                    20*

18*        19*

3*

2*

1*

### *Flower Notes: Color by Counts*

Using the code, make this flower come to life in brilliant color.

Whole note = orange
Half note = yellow
Quarter note = red
Eighth note = dark green
Sixteenth note = light green
Quarter rest = pink

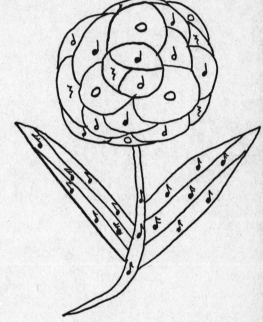

### *Holiday Composer Names*

T    (Tchaikovsky)
H    (Haydn)
A    (Albeniz)
N    (Nielson)
K    (Kuhlau)
S    (Stravinsky)
G    (Grofe)
I    (Ives)
V    (Verdi)
I    (Ibert)
N    (Nardini)
G    (Grieg)

Find names of composers for each letter of this holiday.

## Musical Instruments: Word Search

```
C Y M B A L S M O A L O S X
A O R N O O P I C C O L O C
W I M U P U R S T Y O L T D
S T R U M P E T U L F E G R
S T O B H R E R E A R C L U
B U S T A R E I N V E N T M
A B A R R C L A R I N E T A
S A X O P H O N E O C O O P
N S Y M I I P G C L H A R P
A S L B A M I L E I H E A X
R O O O N E A E L N O G H T
E O R N O S M E L A R T I E
X N B E L L S A I T N E R E
O N T H E T O B O E N Y T S
```

The following words are hidden above: bassoon, bells, cello, chimes, clarinet, cymbal, flute, drum, French horn, harp, oboe, piano, piccolo, saxophone, snare, triangle, trombone, trumpet, tuba, violin.

## Music in Harmony: Word Search

```
F L A T T O N I C
M E L O D Y L M A
U M S N C H O R D
S I E T R I A D E
I N V E R S I O N
C O E P Z T H S C
I R N I S E A C E
A O T K J P R A M
N W H S P Z M L A
A T O N A L O E J
S H A R P C N A O
A M I N O R Y E R
```

The following words are hidden above: atonal, cadence, chord, flat, harmony, inversion, major, melody, minor, musician, row, scale, seventh, sharp, skip, step, tonic, triad.

## Orchestral Instruments: Crossword Puzzle

*Across:*

1. High woodwind
5. High double-reed
6. Also called a fiddle
7. Low double-reed
10. Percussion

*Down:*

2. Brass with slide
3. Keyboard instrument
4. Between a viola and string bass
6. Lower than a violin
8. String instrument of angels
9. Bass horn

## Folk Instruments: Crossword Puzzle

*Across:*

1. Wind instrument with a keyboard
2. The lowest sounding homemade instrument
6. A wind instrument held close to the mouth
9. An ancient string instrument
10. A five-stringed _____
11. A pair of these is fine for rhythm

*Down:*

1. A string instrument for playing harmonies
3. Also known as a violin
4. Associated with the Hawaiian Islands
5. A stringed instrument akin to ancient lute
6. Played by angels
7. A favorite with cowboys
8. Also used for cutting boards

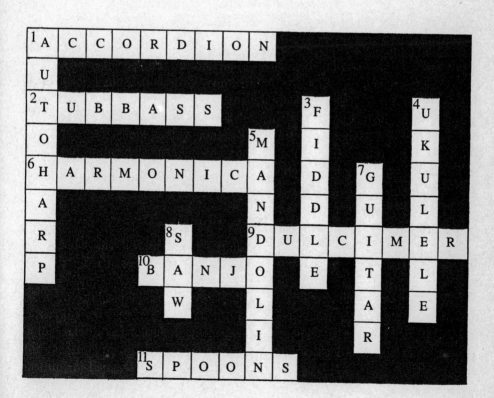

# Appendix

## BOOKS FOR STUDENT USE

Bakeless, Katherine. *Storylives of Great Composers*. J.B. Lippincott Co., Philadelphia, 1953.

Balet, John B. *What Makes an Orchestra?* Walck Publishers, New York.

Commins, Dorothy. *All About the Symphony Orchestra*. Random House, New York, 1960.

Craig, Jean. *The Heart of the Orchestra*. Lerner Publications, Minneapolis, 1962.

Davis, Lionel and Edith. *The Story of the Piano*. Lerner Publications, Minneapolis, 1963.

Deucher, Sybil. *Brahms, the Young*. E.P. Dutton & Co., New York, 1946.

Deucher, Sybil. *Edvard Grieg, Boy of the Northland*. E.P. Dutton & Co., New York, 1946.

Ewen, David. *Leonard Bernstein, Biography for Young People*. Chilton Publishing Co.,

Fox, Sidney, and MacClusky, Thomas. *The World of Popular Music, Rock*. Follett Publishing Co., Chicago, 1973.

Goss, M.B. *Deep-Flowing Brook. The Story of Bach*. Henry Holt & Co., New York.

Grier, Gene. *The Conceptual Approach to Rock Music*. Charter Publications, Inc., Valley Forge, Penn. 1974.

Gullan, Marjorie. *The Speech Choir*. Harper & Brothers, New York, 1937.

Kaufman, Helen L. *History's 100 Great Composers*. Grossett & Dunlap, Inc., 1957.

Keefe, Mildred Jones. *Choric Interludes*. Books for Libraries Press, Freeport, New York, 1942.

Kettelkamp, Larry. *Flutes, Whistles & Reeds*. Wm. Morrow & Co., New York, 1962.

Kettelkamp, Larry. *Singing Strings*. Wm. Morrow & Co., New York, 1958.

Posell, Elsa. *This is an Orchestra*. Houghton Mifflin Co., Boston, 1950.

Stoddard, Hope. *From These Comes Music*. Crowell Publishers, New York.

Tetzlaff, Daniel B. *Shining Brass, The Story of the Trumpet and Other Brass Instruments*. Lerner Publications, Minneapolis, 1963.

Watts, Franklin, *Peter and the Wolf, Prokofieff.* Franklin Watts, Inc., New York, 1961.

Wheeler, Opal. *Adventures of Richard Wagner.* E.P. Dutton & Co., New York.

Wheeler, Opal. *Curtain Calls for Schubert.* E.P. Dutton & Co., New York.

Wheeler, Opal. *Frederic Chopin, Son of Poland, Early Years.* E.P. Dutton & Co., New York.

Wheeler, Opal. *Frederic Chopin, Son of Poland, Later Years.* E.P. Dutton & Co., New York.

Wheeler, Opal. *Handel at the Court of Kings.* E.P. Dutton & Co., New York, 1943.

Wheeler, Opal. *The Story of Peter Tchaikowsy.* E.P. Dutton & Co., New York 1953.

Wheeler, Opal, and Deucher. *Edward MacDowell and His Cabin in the Pines.* E.P. Dutton & Co., New York.

Wheeler, Opal, and Deucher. *Franz Schubert and His Merry Friends.* E.P Dutton & Co., New York.

Wheeler, Opal, and Deucher. *Joseph Haydn, The Merry Little Peasant.* E.P. Dutton & Co., New York, 1936.

Wheeler, Opal, and Deucher. *Mozart, the Wonder Boy.* E.P. Dutton & Co., New York, 1936

Wheeler, Opal, and Deucher. *Sebastian Bach, The Boy from Thuringen.* E.P. Dutton & Co., New York, 1962.

Wheeler, Opal and Deucher, *Stephen Foster and His Little Dog Tray.* E.P. Dutton & Co., New York, 1941.

Young, Percy M. *Masters of Music, Handel, Haydn and Others.* David White Inc., 1969.

## BOOKS FOR TEACHER REFERENCE

Ashley, Rosalind Minor. *Activities for Motivating and Teaching Bright Children.* Parker Publishing Company, Inc., West Nyack, N.Y., 1973.

Athey, Margaret and Hotchkiss, Gwen. *A Galaxy of Games for the Music Class.* Parker Publishing Company, Inc., West Nyack, N.Y., 1975.

Bahner, John M. *Individually Guided Education, Learning Styles.* Training Program Institute for Development of Educational Activities, Inc., Melbourne, Florida, 1971

Bennett, Michael. *Pop Hits Listening Guides.* Pop Hits Publishing Co., 1974.

Bennett, Michael. *Surviving in General Music.* Pop Hits Publishing Co., Memphis, Tenn., 1974.

Berchard, Dr. Joseph E. *The Process of Small Groups.* Edutronics Corporation, 1971.

Chartoneau, Margaret, and Winch, Florence. *Experience in Music*. Musical Activities, Media Associates, Camillus, New York, 1973.

Eurich, Alvin C. *Reforming American Education*. Harper & Row, 1972.

Fliegler, Louis A. *A Curriculum Planning for the Gifted*. Prentice Hall, Inc., Englewood Cliffs, N.J., 1961.

Furth, Hans G., and Wachs, Harry. *Thinking Goes to School, Piaget's Theory in Practice*. Oxford University Press, New York, 1974.

Glasser, Joyce Fern. *The Elementary School Learning Center for Independent Study*. Parker Publishing Company, Inc., West Nyack, N.Y., 1971.

Graham, Richard M. *Music for the Exceptional Child*. Music Education National Conference, Reston, Virginia, 1975.

Jackson, Pat. *The Writer's Lap*. Educational Associates, Inc., Fort Lauderdale, Florida, 1971.

Jones, Dr. Richard V. *Learning Activity Packages, An Approach to Individualized Instruction*. Edutronics Corporation, Fort Lauderdale, Florida, 1971.

Johnson, Stuart & Rita. *Designing Individual Instruction Materials*. Westinghouse Learning Press, Berkeley Calif.

Landon, Joseph. *How to Write Learning Activity Packages for Music Educators*. Educational Media Press, Costa Mesa, Calif., 1973.

Malm, William P. *Music Cultures of the Pacific, the Near East and Asia*. History of Music Series, Prentice-Hall, Inc., Englewood Cliffs, N.J., 1967.

Mayer, Robert F. *Developing Attitudes Toward Learning*. Feron Publishing Company.

McNeil, J.H. *Some Guidelines for Small Group Discussion*. Edutronics Corporation, Fort Lauderdale, Florida, 1971.

Meske, Eunice Boardman, and Rinehart, Carroll. *Individualized Instruction in Music*. Music Educators National Conference, Center for Educational Associates, Reston, Virginia, 1975.

Monsour, Sally. *Music in Open Education*. Center for Applied Research, 1974.

Neaderhiser, George. *Comprehensive Music Curriculum*. Kansas State Department of Education, Topeka, Kansas, 1972.

Nettl, Bruno, *Folk and Traditional Music of Western Continents*. History of Music Series, Prentice Hall, Inc., Englewood Cliffs, N.J., 1965.

Shawnee Mission Public Schools. *Individualized Music Curriculum Guide*. Shawnee Mission District 512, Shawnee Mission, Kansas, 1973.

Shawnee Mission Public Schools. *Elementary Music Curriculum Guide*. Shawnee Mission Public Schools 512, Shawnee Mission Kansas, 1972.

Sidnell, Robert. *Building Instructional Programs in Music Education*. Prentice-Hall, Inc., Englewood Cliffs, N.J., 1973.

Thomas, Ronald. *Manhattanville Music Curriculum Program Synthesis*. Media, Inc., Eldora, New York, 1971.

## ARTICLES FOR TEACHER REFERENCE

Barth, Roland. "First We Start with Some Different Assumptions." *Music Educators Journal*, April, 1974.

Benner, Charles. "Music Education in a Changing Society." *Music Educators Journal*, May, 1975.

Guenther, Annette. "Open Education Places the Arts in the Core of the Curriculum." *Music Educators Journal*, April, 1974.

Haynes, Carrie. "Grape Street Elementary School, Los Angeles." *Music Educators Journal*, April, 1974.

Kunhardt, Barbara. "Shady Hill School, Cambridge, Massachusetts." *Music Educators Journal*, April, 1974.

Landon, Joseph. "Strategies for Opening the Traditional Classroom." *Music Educators Journal*, April, 1974.

Moore, Floy S. "Today I Go to Studio K." *Music Educators Journal*, March, 1976.

O'Brien, James. "Freedom to Learn to Teach." *Music Educators Journal*, May, 1974.

Peotter, Jean. "Contracts." *Music Educators Journal*, February, 1975.

Rathbone, Charles. "No Longer Just a Knowledge Pusher." *Music Educators Journal*, April 1974.

Rausch, Kathy. "Olive School, Arlington Heights, Illinois." *Music Educators Journal*, April, 1974.

Regelski, Thomas. "A Ride on the Dialectic Seesaw." *Music Educators Journal*, March, 1975.

Rogers, Vincent. "Open Education: Where Is It Now? Where Is It Heading?" *Music Educators Journal*, April, 1974.

Spodeck, Bernard. "Preparing Music Teachers for Open Education." *Music Educators Journal*, April, 1974.

Springer, Virginia. "Campus Laboratory School, Cutland, New York." *Music Educators Journal*, April, 1974.

*Our woods would be very silent if no
birds sang there except those that
sing the best.*

Thoreau

# Index